Field Guide to
STAINS

How to Identify and Remove
Virtually Every Stain
Known to Man

*By Virginia M. Friedman, Melissa Wagner,
and Nancy Armstrong*

D1007287

QUIRK BOOKS
PHILADELPHIA

DISCLAIMER

Stains come in all shapes, sizes, and types, and addressing all possible variables when recommending removal tips is difficult. While every care has been taken to test the effectiveness of the information in this book, the author and publisher cannot guarantee results nor take responsibility for any damage resulting from any stain removal method.

Copyright © 2002 by Quirk Productions, Inc.
All rights reserved. No part of this book may be reproduced in any form without written permission from the publisher.

Library of Congress Cataloging in Publication Number: 2002104065

ISBN: 1-931686-07-6

Printed in Singapore

Typeset in Adobe Garamond, Franklin Gothic, and Impact

Designed by Susan Van Horn

All photographs copyright © 2002 by Quirk Productions, Inc.

Distributed in North America by Chronicle Books
85 Second Street
San Francisco, CA 94105

10 9 8 7 6

Quirk Books
215 Church Street
Philadelphia, PA 19106
www.quirkbooks.com

Contents

Field Guide to Stains

FRUITS AND VEGETABLES

MEAT AND PROTEIN

DAIRY PRODUCTS

SAUCES AND CONDIMENTS

BEVERAGES

HOUSEHOLD ITEMS AND MISCELLANY

GARAGE AND YARD

BODILY FUNCTIONS

BATHROOM AND BEAUTY PRODUCTS

OFFICE AND SCHOOL PRODUCTS

Introduction

Whoever coined the phrase "good, clean fun" obviously wasn't thinking of eating a rocky-road ice-cream cone while wearing a white T-shirt on a hot, summer day. "Fun" is often synonymous with "messy," and this book is written for fun-loving people such as yourself. *Field Guide to Stains* is the perfect companion for those of us who've ever had lapses of eye-hand coordination at the dinner table, in the garage, bathroom, or elsewhere. We may not be able to teach you grace, but perhaps we can help keep you a little cleaner.

With tips on how to remove more than 100 spills and smudges, this is the ultimate book on filth and how to get rid of it. Most stains don't talk, so we've included tips on how to identify an array of spots. Turn to the sections How to Identify Your Stain and the Color Guide to Stains to start playing the elimination game. Once you've determined the culprit, locate the stain removal method in the *Field Guide,* which is conveniently organized by the sources of stains: Fruits and Vegetables, Meat and Protein, Dairy Products, Sauces and Condiments, Office and School Products, and so forth. You get the idea. Even Lady Macbeth and Monica Lewinsky could find solutions to their "damned spots." If you're uncertain about specific terms or products mentioned in the book, look them up in the Glossary in the back of the book. We told you this was comprehensive, didn't we?

And if all else fails, prop the book up under your chin before that next bite of lasagna!

• Use the icon key on page 4 of the color insert for an at-a-glance guide to typical stain seasons, areas of occurrence, and removal techniques. The numbered camera icon refers to the color plate section.

Stain Removal Tips

☒ Read garment labels before treating any stain.

☒ Use cleaning products according to manufacturer's labels.

☒ Apply stain removers and solutions to the back of a stain; this will push the stain out of the fabric instead of into it.

☒ Treat the stain until it is removed, then discontinue treatment.

☒ Do not apply any kind of heat (including ironing and using the dryer) until you are certain that the stain has been removed. Heat will often set a stain and make it difficult to remove. Instead, allow garments to air dry, then treat again, if needed. Drying stained garments in sunlight is best; it provides some mild bleaching.

☒ Testing for colorfastness is recommended before using any kind of bleach or strong cleaning product. To test, apply the cleaning agent to an inconspicuous area of the garment, such as an inside seam. Steps that include bleaching and may require such a test are indicated in the margin by the universal symbol for bleach, a triangle.

☒ If you have to take a garment to the dry cleaners, point out the stain and explain what it is so that it can be treated accordingly.

☒ Make sure that flammable materials such as turpentine and acetone are completely rinsed from a garment before putting it in the dryer.

How to Identify Your Stain

Take the guesswork out of stain identification by asking yourself the following questions:

"When did I last wear this?" Narrowing down the time and place where the stain was acquired will help you figure out just what was spilled.

"How could the stain have happened?" Did you sit in it, brush against it, or maybe scuff it with a pant leg? Connecting cause with effect is essential; often, placement of the stain will help identify those mysterious ones.

"What color is it?" One of the easiest ways to identify a stain is by its color. But be aware, some stains react differently to different-colored fabrics, while some, like oil, appear colorless at first but darken as dirt clings to them. For help identifying possible sources of colored stains, see the first pages of the color section.

"What does this smell like?" Some stains, like alcohol, fruit juices, or motor oil, have unmistakable odors, especially before washing.

Fruits and Vegetables

1.   **AVOCADO**

General
Description:

A tropical fruit (Persea americana) *with a single large pit, spherical to pear shaped, smooth to rough-textured skin with a green to purplish color, and yellow to green flesh with a buttery texture and high unsaturated fat content; generally used like a vegetable and consumed raw; also known as an alligator pear.* Avocados have enjoyed an increased visibility in recent years with the widespread popularity of Mexican cuisine. The word "avocado" comes from the Spanish word *aguacate,* which in turn derives from the ancient Aztec word *āhuacatl,* meaning "testicle." Avocados are grown throughout South and Central America and in California, and they have the highest fat content of any fruit.

Season:

Avocados are a source of stains during any season, but especially the summer barbecue season and at winter and summer sporting events, where guacamole is a popular dip for chips.

Areas of
Occurrence:

Avocado stains normally occur in the standard food-stain places—the fronts of blouses, shirts, and sweaters, and the lap areas of pants, jeans, and dresses. Particularly clumsy or careless people may also find these stains on the seats of their pants, if they don't look before sitting in an "unoccupied" chair.

Time of Occurrence:	Avocados are popular in salads and sandwiches and "wraps" often associated with lunch fare, as well as in sauces and dips that are commonly eaten as snacks in the afternoon or evening.
Variations of Significance:	Guacamole; any sandwich or "wrap" with "California" in the name

REMOVAL:

1. Use a dull knife or spoon to remove as much as possible.

2. Rub the stain with a liquid enzyme detergent and let stand several minutes, then soak the stain in cold water for 10 to 15 minutes, or until the stain is loosened. Occasionally rub the stained material between thumbs during soaking. Rinse well. Repeat until you have removed as much as possible.

 3. If the stain remains, apply a laundry presoak (spot stain remover) and let stand several minutes.

 4. Launder in the hottest water safe for the fabric.

2. ## BABY FOOD

General
Description:

Food with a runny, mashed, no-chewing-necessary consistency, made especially for babies who are just beginning to eat whole food rather than milk. Baby food can be made from just about any fruit or vegetable. Some popular varieties in the United States and Europe include apple, banana, and carrots. In Japan, Gerber's top-selling baby-food flavor is sardine.

Season:

Babies must eat year-round, so baby-food stains can happen during any season.

Areas of
Occurrence:

A baby-food stain is frequently found on clothing that surrounds the neck, arms, or chest of the supervising adult. The splatter can range as far away as your back, pants, or socks, depending upon the projectile speed and direction in which the baby flings the food. The baby will most likely be covered in the stuff—the bib, intended to catch most of the food, often ends up being cast aside by the child early in the process, making it one of the cleaner garments. In these cases, baby's dress, shirt, or jumper collects most of the mess.

Time of
Occurrence:

By the time a baby starts eating these more-solid foods, parents are working toward getting the baby on a standard breakfast, lunch, and dinner routine. Baby-food stains will occur during these times, unless the child is particularly obstinate and the parents are indulgent—

then there is no telling when this stain might appear.

REMOVAL: 1. Use a dull knife or spoon to remove as much as possible.

2. For fresh stains, soak and agitate the fabric thoroughly in cold water. For dried stains, soak fabric in a mixture of cold water and liquid enzyme detergent for 30 minutes or longer, until the stain is loosened. Rinse well.

3. If the stain remains, rub undiluted liquid enzyme detergent into the stain and let stand several minutes.

 4. Launder according to garment label.

5. If the stain remains, soak in enzyme detergent mixture and cold water up to 30 minutes again.

 6. Apply a laundry presoak (spot stain remover) and launder again. On white fabrics, bleach any remaining stain by blotting with lemon juice and setting to dry in the sunlight.

3.   **BAKED BEANS**

General
Description:
A dish consisting of cooked navy or great northern beans, pork, onion, molasses or brown sugar, and seasonings. Baked beans are an extremely popular dish in Great Britain. The British, according to surveys, consume twice as many baked beans per capita than Americans do, possibly because baked beans are acceptable at every meal—including and especially breakfast—in Great Britain. Baked beans are a favorite at summer picnics and barbecues around the globe.

Season:
Baked beans are most popular in the summertime. You almost always find a crock of baked beans next to the potato salad and corn on the cob at picnics and barbecues during the summer holidays.

Areas of
Occurrence:

Stains from baked beans normally occur in the standard food-stain areas—in trails on the fronts of blouses, T-shirts, golf shirts, or dresses, and the lap areas of shorts, jeans, and skirts.

Time of
Occurrence:
Picnics and barbecues, the riskiest times for acquiring this stain, usually take place during the afternoon and early evening hours. However, leftover beans can cause problems late into the night.

REMOVAL: 1.   **Use a dull knife or spoon to remove as much as possible.**

2. Flush the back of the stain immediately with cold water to force the stain through fabric.

3. Rub a liquid enzyme detergent into the stain and let stand several minutes. Rub the fabric between thumbs, then rinse well.

4. Sponge with a mild bleach, such as white vinegar, hydrogen peroxide, or lemon juice, then rinse well.

5. Repeat steps 3 and 4 until no more stain can be removed.

6. Apply a laundry presoak (spot stain remover) and let stand several minutes.

7. Launder with an enzyme detergent. Let garment dry in the sun for added bleaching.

8. If the stain remains, rub an enzyme detergent into the stain and then soak garment in warm water for up to 30 minutes, or until the stain is gone. Rinse well.

9. If the stain remains, apply laundry presoak (spot stain remover) and relaunder.

4. **BEET**

General
Description:

Commonly known as the garden beet, this firm, bulbous edible root vegetable (Beta vulgaris) *has leafy green tops, which are also edible and highly nutritious; its color is typically garnet red but can range from pinkish-white to deep red. Also known as* red beet *and* beetroot *(especially in Great Britain).* When cut open, the beet reminded early cooks of a bleeding animal, so was called "beet," derived from the French word *bête,* meaning "beast."

Season:

Beets are available year-round, at salad bars, cafeterias, and restaurants everywhere, and especially in Grandma's kitchen, when she cooks foods from the Old Country.

Areas of
Occurrence:

The chest and lap areas of Sunday-best attire are common for this stain—many churchgoers find beets a tempting commodity at Sunday afternoon salad bars or at the dinner table at Grandma's house.

Time of
Occurrence:

Beet stains rarely occur at any time other than between 12:00 P.M. and 2:00 P.M. or from 5:00 P.M. to 7:00 P.M.

Variations of
Significance:

Borscht; pickled beets

REMOVAL:

1. Use a dull knife or spoon to remove as much as possible.

2. Soak a slice of white bread in cold water, then lay it on the stain to absorb the beet juice. Turn the bread over once it is saturated or replace it with another slice of bread.

3. Once the bread has absorbed as much stain as possible, rinse garment with cold water.

4. Apply laundry presoak (spot stain remover) and let stand several minutes.

5. Launder with enzyme detergent according to garment label.

6. If the stain remains, dilute bleach as directed on label and soak the stained garment in it in a nonmetal container for 6 to 8 hours or until the stain is removed. Check first for colorfastness. If color is affected, spread garment over a container in the sink and let cold water slowly drip onto the stain. Drain the container as needed. Continue for 3 to 4 hours.

7. If the stain remains, sponge with equal parts hydrogen peroxide and water and lay garment in the sun. Keep moist with peroxide solution until the stain is gone. Test first for colorfastness.

8. Rinse well and launder according to garment label.

5.   **BROCCOLI**

General
Description:

Italian for "cabbage sprout"; a member of the cabbage family (Brassica oleracea) *with a tight cluster (called a curd) of emerald green florets atop a stout, paler green edible stalk and dark green leaves.* Broccoli is much maligned by children and even some adults—former U.S. President George Bush refused to eat the vegetable. But broccoli is loved by at least as many people as those who hate it. One historic broccoli lover, Drusus Caesar, son of the Roman emperor Tiberius, appreciated it so much that he ate little else for more than a month. He stopped when his urine turned green.

Season:

Broccoli can be found at any time of year in take-out Chinese food, homemade casseroles, and any number of other dishes—even as a topping on pizza. The broccoli stain is not limited by season.

Areas of
Occurrence:

A difficult stain to acquire, it is most likely found on the seat of your pants or possibly on the elbow or forearm of a shirt or blouse, if the broccoli is cooked to the point of mushiness. Nutritionists recommend serving broccoli while it is still crisp to preserve essential vitamins and minerals. Therefore, you are more likely to be stained by something coating the broccoli than by the vegetable itself.

| Time of Occurrence: | Because broccoli probably will not stain unless it is cooked, you will generally get this stain only at meal times, traditionally in the early afternoon or evening. |

Variations of Significance: Casserole; gourmet pizza; stir-fry

REMOVAL:

1. Use a dull knife or spoon to remove as much as possible.

2. Rinse the stain well with cold water.

3. Rub the stain with a liquid enzyme detergent and let garment stand several minutes.

4. Soak in cold water, rubbing the fabric occasionally between your thumbs. Continue soaking and rubbing until you have removed as much stain as possible.

5. Rinse well.

6. If the stain remains, apply a laundry presoak (spot stain remover) and let stand several minutes.

7. Launder according to garment label.

6.   **CABBAGE, RED**

General
Desciption:

A variety of the green cabbage (Brassica oleracea capitata), *red cabbage is usually small, with dark red-purple waxy leaves that are tougher and slightly more bitter than those of the green cabbage.* Red cabbage is a staple in tossed salads, both at home and at restaurants. Baseball player Babe Ruth wore a cabbage leaf under his cap for luck while playing baseball—he changed it every two innings.

Season:

You run the biggest risk of acquiring such a stain when cutting and preparing cabbage—once it has had the chance to dry out a little, it will rarely cause any problem. Salads including red cabbage are a popular cuisine during the hot summer months, when appetites are small and hemlines are high. The month of January also has the potential for red cabbage stains, especially if a New Year's resolution includes dieting.

Areas of
Occurrence:

The forearms and waist areas of shirts and blouses and the fronts of aprons are at greatest risk from a red cabbage stain, as it is most likely acquired when cutting the cabbage head. Other garments have a slim chance of acquiring such a stain, usually transmitted by fingers and hands covered in the juices thoughtlessly brushing the sides of pants or some other piece of clothing.

Variations of
Significance: Coleslaw; salads

REMOVAL: 1.   Use a dull knife or spoon to remove as much as possible.

 2.   Rinse the stain well with cold water.

 3.   Rub the stain with a liquid enzyme detergent and let stand several minutes. Do not be alarmed if the stain changes color.

4.   Soak garment in cold water, rubbing occasionally between your thumbs. Continue soaking and rubbing until you have removed as much stain as possible.

 5.   Rinse well.

 6.   If the stain remains, apply a laundry presoak (spot stain remover) and let stand several minutes.

 7.   Launder according to garment label.

7.   **CARROT**

General
Description:
A member of the parsley family (Daucus carota)*; has lacy green foliage, an edible orange, purple, yellow, or white taproot with a mild, sweet flavor and crisp texture; has a tapering shape and comes in a variety of sizes.* Regardless of the myth popularized by the cartoon rabbit Bugs Bunny, wild rabbits do not eat carrots. Ironically, Mel Blanc—the voice of Bugs Bunny— was allergic to carrots.

Season: Carrot is an ingredient in many foods that are served in any season, including stews and salads. They can also be served on their own as the vegetable portion of dinner or as a snack.

Areas of
Occurrence:

Carrot stains are difficult to acquire. Nutritionists recommend serving carrots while they are still crisp, to preserve essential vitamins and minerals. Thus, when carrots are cooked whole or served raw, you are more likely to be stained by something coating the carrot than by the vegetable itself. Exceptions are when carrots are served as baby food (see Baby Food on page 6) and are pureed for soups, sauces, or juices. They are then most likely found on the seat of your pants or possibly on the elbow or forearm of a shirt or blouse.

| Variations of Significance: | Carrot cake; coleslaw; salads; soups |

REMOVAL

1. Use a dull knife or spoon to remove as much as possible.

2. Rinse the stain well with cold water.

3. Rub the stain with a liquid enzyme detergent and let stand several minutes.

4. Soak garment in cold water, rubbing the stain occasionally between your thumbs. Continue soaking and rubbing until you have removed as much stain as possible.

5. Rinse well.

6. If the stain remains, apply a laundry presoak (spot stain remover) and let stand several minutes.

7. Launder according to garment label.

---

8. **FRUITS OR BERRIES**

| General Description: | Fruits: *The edible organs that develop from the ovary of flowering plants; contain one or more seeds; usually sweet and eaten as is or processed into other foods.* |

Berry: *Imprecisely used term to describe any small, juicy fruit that grows on a vine or bush and generally has a thin skin, multiple small to tiny seeds, and a sweet flavor.* Fruits and berries comprise any number of foods, such as peaches, pears, apples, strawberries, blueberries, raspberries, blackberries, oranges, grapes, melons, plums, pomegranates, and cranberries. Botanically speaking, a "true" berry has seeds on the inside, not on the outside. Therefore, "true" berries include the grape, tomato, and eggplant but not the raspberry, blackberry, or strawberry. For our purposes, this category of stain encompasses all varieties commonly referred to as "fruits" or "berries," regardless of exact definition.

Season: You cannot relax your vigilance against this stain in any particular season, as you may encounter the juice or flesh of a fruit or berry at any time of year. There is an increased chance of stain during summer, when numerous fruits and berries are in season locally, depending on your climate. Fruits and berries play a more prominent role in desserts, entrees, and snacks (and as a staining agent) during these hot months.

Time of Occurrence: Fruits and berries are eaten throughout the day, and can therefore stain at any time. Pay careful attention when sipping juice, putting berries on cereal, or eating grapefruit at breakfast, when snacking on an apple, orange, or bunch of grapes to boost energy midday, or when devouring a strawberry or cherry pie for dessert after dinner.

Variations of Significance:	Desserts, especially in pies, cobblers, and over ice cream; juices; in some entrees and soups; on cheese plates; wine (see WINE, RED on page 119; WINE, WHITE on page 122)

REMOVAL: *For fresh stains on fabric:*

1. Treat the stain as soon as possible. Use a dull knife or spoon to remove as much as possible. If you cannot treat the stain immediately, sprinkle it with salt.

2. Rinse any remaining stain well with cold water.

3. Rub liquid laundry detergent into the stain. Do not use bar or natural soap of any kind on the fabric or the stain will set.

4. Let stand several minutes, then rinse the back of the stain well in hot water, letting the water pass quickly through the fabric.

5. If the stain remains, stretch the stained fabric stain-side down over a basin. Boil three or more cups of water in a pot or teakettle and carefully pour over the stain from a height of 1 to 2 feet. (This may require two people: one to hold the fabric taut and the other to pour the water.) This procedure will force the stain through the fabric. If you're the only one on stain duty, run the faucet water as hot as possible and carefully hold the stain under it.

6. If the stain remains, apply a laundry presoak (spot stain remover) and launder with liquid enzyme detergent.

7. If the stain remains, sponge it with a light bleach solution, such as equal parts white vinegar and water. Rinse well and let dry in sunlight. Repeat as needed until no more stain can be removed.

8. Apply laundry presoak and relaunder with enzyme detergent.

9. If the stain remains, rub enzyme detergent into the stain and soak in water up to one hour or until the stain is removed. Rinse well and launder.

For dried stains on fabric:

1. Make a paste of borax and water (at a ratio of approximately 3 to 1) and spread onto the stain.

2. Let stand 15 minutes, then rinse. If borax is not available, rub glycerin into the stain and let stand for one hour. Rinse.

3. See steps 3 through 9 for fresh stains, above.

9. **JAM OR JELLY**

General
Description:
Jam: *A preserve of slightly crushed fruit boiled with sugar.*
Jelly: *A sweet spread of fruit juice boiled with sugar and
sometimes pectin, then cooled to a soft, sticky consistency.*
The primary difference between a jam and a jelly is that
a jam has fruit bits in it, since the whole fruit is boiled
for preparation. Popular varieties of these breakfast treats
include grape, strawberry, and orange marmalade.

Season:

Jam and jelly are preserved, so these stains aren't limited
to summer, when most fruits and berries are available.
Jam-filled cookies and cakes may be more common
during the winter holiday season, but jam itself is a stain
source you'll find year round.

Areas of
Occurrence:

The front of a blouse, jacket, or pair of pants is the
most likely spot you'll encounter this stain. Jam and jelly
have a particularly plop-prone consistency, thus there is
little chance of escaping this stain once the substance
has been set in motion.

Time of
Occurrence:
The most common time of day for this stain is probably
morning, at breakfast, though lunchtime and dessert are
also popular times to consume this sweet treat.

Variations of
Significance:
Peanut butter and jelly sandwiches; jam-filled cookies
and cakes

REMOVAL: *For fresh stains on fabric:*

1. Treat the stain as soon as possible. Use a dull knife or spoon to remove as much as possible. If you cannot treat the stain immediately, sprinkle it with salt.

2. Rinse any remaining stain well with cold water.

3. Rub liquid laundry detergent into the stain. Do not use bar or natural soap of any kind on the fabric or the stain will set.

4. Let stand several minutes, then rinse the back of the stain well in hot water, letting the water pass quickly through the fabric.

5. If the stain remains, stretch the stained fabric stain-side down over a basin. Boil three or more cups of water in a pot or teakettle and carefully pour over the stain from a height of 1 to 2 feet. (This may require two people: one to hold the fabric taut and the other to pour the water.) This procedure will force the stain through the fabric. If you're the only one on stain duty, run the faucet water as hot as possible and carefully hold the stain under it.

6. If the stain remains, apply a laundry presoak (spot stain remover) and launder with liquid enzyme detergent.

7. If the stain remains, sponge the stain with a light bleach solution, such as equal parts white vinegar and water. Rinse well and let dry in sunlight. Repeat as needed until no more stain can be removed.

8. Apply laundry presoak and relaunder with enzyme detergent.

9. If the stain remains, rub enzyme detergent into the stain and soak in water up to 1 hour, or until the stain is removed. Rinse well and launder.

For dried stains on fabric:

1. Make a paste of borax and water (at a ratio of approximately 3 to 1) and spread onto the stain.

2. Let stand 15 minutes, then rinse. If borax is not available, rub glycerin into the stain and let stand for 1 hour. Rinse.

3. See steps 3 through 9 for fresh stains, above.

10. 📷   **LEMON JUICE**

General
Description:

The juice of the yellowish, acidic fruit of a subtropical citrus tree. Lemon juice is useful not only as a food item or flavoring; it can be used to lighten hair in the summertime. In addition to being a source of stains, it also works as a stain-removing agent. It can be used to get rid of lipstick stains on white or colored garments, though it must be diluted with water for this purpose. (See LIPSTICK on page 228.)

Season:
☼

While lemon juice is used as a flavoring in recipes throughout the year, summer is the most likely time for this stain to appear. Fish and seafood are generally served in summer with a lemon wedge, and lemonade is a favorite summertime refreshment. As previously mentioned, lemon juice is a natural hair-lightener when applied on a hot, sunny day.

Areas of
Occurrence:

Juice from a squeezed lemon can squirt just about anywhere, from your eyes to your shoes. Therefore, these stains are not limited to any specific area of clothing, though perhaps the front and sleeves of a blouse or T-shirt are the most vulnerable.

Variations of
Significance:

Fish and seafood condiment; lemonade; vinaigrette

REMOVAL: *On fabric:*

1. Rinse the back of the stain immediately and thoroughly with cold water to neutralize the acid.

2. Place garment on an absorbent cloth and sponge well with ammonia, starting from the outside of the stain edge. Replace cloth underneath as it becomes saturated. (If treating stains on wool or silk, dilute ammonia with an equal amount of cold water.) If ammonia is not available, substitute a baking soda paste, mixing baking soda and water (at a ratio of approximately 3 to 1). Rub into the stain.

3. Rinse well.

4. Repeat as needed.

5. Launder according to garment label.

On carpet:

1. Sponge the stain immediately with cold water to remove as much acid as possible.

2. Mix baking soda and water to make a paste (at a ratio of approximately 3 to 1) and rub onto the stain. Scrub into carpet with an old toothbrush, then let dry.

3. **Repeat steps 1 and 2 until you have removed as much stain as possible.**

4. **Vacuum.**

---

11.   **ONION, RED**

General
Description:

A plant in the amaryllis family having an edible, pungent bulb that is a staple in all kinds of cookery. Commonly used in savory dishes for flavor, red onions are found on most menus, in dishes ranging from salads to burritos. Their flavor comes largely from their aroma; an apple, onion, and potato all have the same taste, but the difference is in their smells. To prove this, perform a taste test: Pinch your nose and take a bite of each; they all taste sweet.

Season:

Since red onions are most common in warm-weather foods, such as pasta salad and salsa fresca, this stain is more prevalent in summer, especially at barbecues. However, since you may crave a slice on a hamburger in winter, these stains won't be limited to the hot months of the year.

Areas of
Occurrence:

The lap areas of pants, shorts, skirts, and sundresses are the most likely spots for this stain to show up. The fronts of swimsuits and bathing trunks are not exempt, due in large part to the proximity of pools to grills in backyards across the country.

Time of Occurrence:	This is one stain that will almost never appear on clothing early in the morning, though the occasional Spanish omelet might provide the exception to this rule. Lunchtime and evening are the most common times to incur this stain.
Variations of Significance:	Burritos; hambugers; pasta salad; salsa; tacos

REMOVAL:

1. Use a dull knife or spoon to remove as much as possible.

2. Rinse the stain well with cold water.

3. Rub the stain with a liquid enzyme detergent and let stand several minutes. Do not be alarmed if the stain changes color.

4. Soak garment in cold water, rubbing it occasionally between your thumbs. Continue soaking and rubbing until you have removed as much stain as possible.

5. Rinse well.

6. If the stain remains, apply a laundry presoak (spot stain remover) and let stand several minutes.

7. Launder according to garment label.

12.   **PEPPER, RED/GREEN/YELLOW**

General
Description:
The usually green or red fruits of any of several plants belonging to the genus Capsicum, *ranging from mild to very pungent in flavor.* Found in ethnic cuisines as varied as Chinese, Mexican, Italian, and Indian, peppers can actually contain up to six times as much vitamin C as oranges. The highest levels of vitamin C are found in peppers in the "green" stage, and mild peppers contain more than their hot counterparts. The "heat" comes from the alkaloid ingredient capsaicin; spicy peppers contain more of this substance than mild ones. Climate, location, and age determine the amount of capsaicin in a pepper. To grow really hot peppers, the temperature at night must stay warm; the longer a pepper is left on the vine, the more capsaicin it will contain, and the hotter it will be.

Season:

Like onions, peppers are common in summertime foods, such as pasta and green salads, as well as in Mexican treats, such as quesadillas and enchiladas. Given their intense flavor and their popularity as a pizza topping, however, this stain is not limited to summer.

Areas of
Occurrence:

There is not much chance you'll find this stain on the back of a jacket or pair of trousers, though the errant pepper could find its way onto a lawn chair. Again, like onions, pepper stains will most commonly be found on the fronts of T-shirts, shorts, and jeans.

Variations of
Significance: Enchiladas; marinara sauce; stir-fry; salads

REMOVAL: 1. Use a dull knife or spoon to remove as much as possible.

 2. Rinse the stain well with cold water.

3. Rub the stain with a liquid enzyme detergent and let stand several minutes.

4. Soak garment in cold water, rubbing it occasionally between your thumbs. Continue soaking and rubbing until you have removed as much stain as possible.

 5. Rinse well.

 6. If the stain remains, apply a laundry presoak (spot stain remover) and let stand several minutes.

 7. Launder according to garment label.

13.   **POTATO, SWEET**

General
Description: *The sweet, bright-orange-fleshed tuber of fall and winter that grows on the Central American trailing vine* Ipomoea batatas, *a member of the morning glory family.* These

potatoes are tasty when prepared the ways you would prepare white potatoes and winter squash—fried, mashed, roasted, or baked. Although "yam" and "sweet potato" are often used interchangeably, they are, in fact, two entirely different vegetables. Yams have dark, scaly skin, while sweet potatoes have a thin, smooth skin.

Season:

Since this vegetable is at is at its best in fall and winter, these are the seasons you'll find its stain on your clothing. Pies and casseroles made with the tuber will have you wondering what to do with the burnt-orange stain on your favorite woolly sweater.

Areas of Occurrence:

Winter clothing is bulky by nature, thus sweater sleeves often are dragged through bowls of food, especially at crowded family gatherings where there is a veritable cornucopia of foodstuffs. Other common spots to find this stain are the fronts of jeans and corduroys, or the lapels of a casual suit jacket.

Time of Occurrence:

This stain will appear in the evening or late afternoon, when the sun is just going down. There is little chance of a sweet-potato stain occurring in the morning, though leftover pie certainly makes a tasty breakfast.

Variations of Significance:

Potato pancakes; pumpkin and sweet-potato soups; sweet-potato pie

REMOVAL:

1. Use a dull knife or spoon to remove as much as possible.

2. For fresh stains, soak and agitate the fabric thoroughly in cold water. For dried stains, soak fabric in a soapy mixture of cold water and liquid enzyme detergent for 30 minutes or until the stain is loosened. Rinse well.

3. If the stain remains, rub a liquid enzyme detergent into the stain and let stand several minutes.

4. Launder according to garment label.

5. If the stain remains, soak in enzyme detergent and cold water mixture for up to 30 minutes.

6. Apply a laundry presoak (spot stain remover) and launder again. On white fabrics, bleach any remaining stain by blotting with lemon juice and setting to dry in the sunlight.

14. **SPINACH**

General Description: *A plant,* Spinachia oleracea, *of the goosefoot family, cultivated for its crinkly or flat leaves, which are eaten as a vegetable.* One of the first cooking greens to appear in spring, spinach is a vegetable found in the traditional foods of nations around the globe. Although it's true that spinach is rich in iron, it also contains oxalic acid, which binds to the iron, allowing less than 5 percent of it to reach the body. However, spinach is also an excellent source of beta-carotene.

Season: A stain caused by fresh spinach is most likely to occur in spring or summer, but a frozen-spinach stain can happen at any time of year.

Areas of Occurrence: After eating spinach dishes, you may discover a stain anywhere from the fronts and sleeves of shirts to the legs of trousers and fronts of skirts. A more common type of spinach stain, however, occurs when a parent or guardian is feeding creamed or pureed spinach to a baby. In this situation, the green stuff can be found in such far-reaching spots as socks and headbands, or even the insides of garments.

Variations of Significance: Spinach salad; creamed spinach; eggs Florentine; spanakopita

REMOVAL:

1. Use a dull knife or spoon to remove as much as possible.

2. Place garment stain-side down on absorbent cloth and sponge the back of the stain with rubbing alcohol, replacing pad underneath as needed. Test first for colorfastness. (For acetate fabrics, dilute

alcohol with 2 parts water. Do not use alcohol on wool.) Rinse well in cold water.

3. If the stain remains, use an old toothbrush and scrub the stain with non-gel toothpaste (preferably containing baking soda). Let stand for 2 to 3 minutes. Rinse well. If toothpaste is not available, sponge the stain with white vinegar, then rinse well.

4. If the stain remains, repeat steps 1 through 3 until you've removed as much stain as possible.

5. Rub the stain with laundry presoak (spot stain remover) and let stand for several minutes.

6. Launder with a liquid enzyme detergent.

---

15. **SQUASH**

General Description: *The fruit of any of various vinelike, tendril-bearing plants belonging to the genus* Cucurbita, *of the gourd family.* Squash are treated as vegetables in the kitchen. There is some debate regarding where the term "squash" comes from; it could be from the Narraganset *askútasquash*, meaning "green thing eaten green."

Season: Squash is most often considered a summer fruit—hence
   "summer squash"—though there are winter squash
ripening along with pumpkins and sweet potatoes.
Given these seasonal varieties, this is a stain that occurs
primarily in summer and winter.

Variations of   Ratatouille; stir-fry
Significance:

REMOVAL: 1.   Use a dull knife or spoon to remove as much as
possible.

   2.   Rinse the stain well with cold water.

3.   Rub the stain with a liquid enzyme detergent and
let stand several minutes.

4.   Soak garment in cold water, rubbing it occasionally between your thumbs. Continue soaking and
rubbing until you have removed as much stain as
possible.

   5.   Rinse well.

   6.   If the stain remains, apply a laundry presoak (spot
stain remover) and let stand several minutes.

   7.   Launder according to garment label.

16.   **TOMATO**

General
Description:

A large, mildly acid, pulpy berry, red to red-yellow when ripe, eaten raw or cooked as a vegetable. Often though of as a vegetable, the popular tomato is actually a fruit. A fruit is classified as the edible part of the plant that contains the seeds, while a vegetable is the stems, leaves, and root of the plant. Until the late eighteenth century, many cultures, including the British, denied the tomato's existence as a food because it was thought to be poisonous due to its relation to the deadly nightshade. This myth eventually died out among United States colonists, and by the early nineteenth century, tomatoes were a necessary ingredient in Creole cooking as well as seafood dishes from Maine.

Season:

Though the actual growing season for tomatoes is very short—from spring in the American South to mid-fall in the North—the tomato is a staple that is enjoyed throughout the year because it is easily and well preserved in cans. Fresh tomatoes are more likely to stain clothing in the summer, but stewed, pureed, or canned tomatoes will stain all year round.

Areas of
Occurrence:

The juice, pulp, and seeds of the tomato have an unrivaled ability to squirt unexpectedly, landing on unsuspecting clothing and upholstery. Therefore, all clothing is vulnerable to a tomato stain.

Time of Occurrence:	Tomato consumption has no prescribed time. From omelets in the morning to bacon-lettuce-and-tomato sandwiches in the afternoon to an Italian feast in the evening, tomato stains are ubiquitous.
Variations of Significance:	Bruschetta; burritos; chili; gazpacho; jambalaya; marinara sauce; pizza; ratatouille; salads; salsa; tacos; tomato soup

REMOVAL:

1. Use a dull knife or spoon to remove as much as possible.

 2. Flush the back of the stain immediately with cold water to force stain through fabric.

3. Rub a liquid enzyme detergent into the stain and let stand several minutes. Rub the fabric between thumbs, then rinse well.

 4. Sponge with a mild bleach, such as white vinegar, hydrogen peroxide, or lemon juice, then rinse well.

5. Repeat steps 3 and 4 until no more stain can be removed.

 6. Apply a laundry presoak (spot stain remover) and let stand several minutes.

7. Launder with an enzyme detergent. Let garment

dry in the sun for added bleaching.

8. If the stain remains, rub an enzyme detergent into the stain and then soak garment in warm water for up to 30 minutes, or until the stain is gone. Rinse well.

 9. Apply laundry presoak (spot stain remover) and relaunder.

---

17. **ZUCCHINI**

General Description:
A cucumber-shaped summer squash having a smooth, dark green skin. Zucchini, *Cucurbita pepo*, is a member of the cucumber and melon family. This squash is at its best when ripe and firm. Those who choose to plant this squash should check with friends first; zucchini plants produce far more fruit than one family can consume in a summer.

Season:
Since zucchini is a summer squash, the stains from this vegetable invariably appear in the warmest months of the year.

Areas of Occurrence:
 Given this vegetable's popularity at barbecues, and the popularity of spirits at those same barbecues, zucchini stains can appear on any and all areas of clothing, including bathing-suit straps and the seat of a favorite pair of Capri pants.

Variations of   Pasta salads; polenta; ratatouille; stews
Significance:

REMOVAL: 1.   Use a dull knife or spoon to remove as much as possible.

 2.   Rinse the stain well with cold water.

3.   Rub the stain with a liquid enzyme detergent and let stand several minutes.

4.   Soak garment in cold water, rubbing it occasionally between your thumbs. Continue soaking and rubbing until you have removed as much stain as possible.

 5.   Rinse well.

 6.   If the stain remains, apply a laundry presoak (spot stain remover) and let stand several minutes.

 7.   Launder according to garment label.

Meat and Protein

18. **EGG**

General
Description:

The roundish reproductive body produced by the female of certain animals, including birds, consisting of an ovum and its envelope of albumen, jelly, membranes, egg case, or shell, according to species. The chicken egg might just be the most important food in the kitchen, since it contains all nine essential amino acids as well as several vitamins. Many of our favorite foods would be unrecognizable without the egg, from breakfast to desserts to baked goods of all kinds. Though most eggs are white or brown, some breeds of chickens lay other colors of eggs. For example, Ameraucana and Araucana chickens can lay eggs in shades of blue or green.

Season:

Given the incredible edible egg's wide-ranging uses—from sauce thickener to quiche base to pizza topping (in Australia)—you'd be hard-pressed to find a season in which you wouldn't run the risk of an egg stain. Due to the high volume of dessert baking that is done during the holiday seasons, you might encounter this stain more often in November and December.

Areas of
Occurrence:

Since a raw egg is gooey and has the tendency to splash a bit, its stain is likely to be as diverse as its many uses, appearing on both shirts and slacks, as well as aprons,

bibs, skirts, and blazers. Ties, too, are not immune
to this stain, as breakfast before work can be a
hurried affair.

Time of Occurrence:	The aforementioned breakfast is a common time to suffer this stain, though the offense isn't limited to the morning by any means. Since the baking of cookies, cakes, and pies may occur at any time during the hysteria accompanying holiday preparations, an egg stain likewise knows no particular time frame.
Variations of Significance:	Cake and pancake batter; cookie dough; egg salad; frittatas; omelets; pie crust; quiche; salads

REMOVAL:

1. Use a dull knife or spoon to remove as much as possible. Blot remaining stain with an absorbent cloth.

2. Sponge the stain with cold water, then rinse the back of the stain well. Dried stains may need to be loosened by rubbing with a liquid enzyme detergent and soaking in cold water until the stain begins to break down. Rub the stain between your thumbs while soaking. Rinse well.

3. If the stain remains, rub liquid enzyme detergent into the stain again and let stand for several minutes.

4. Launder according to garment label.

19.   **FATS, ANIMAL**

General
Description:
A class of organic nutrients that includes the lipid family of compounds—triglycerides (fats and oils), phospholipids, and sterols. Used principally in the body to store energy from food eaten in excess of need. Animal fats serve an astounding array of purposes. Not only adding flavor to steaks, roasts, hamburgers, and bacon, they are an essential ingredient in crayons and many soaps. Though many dieters try to avoid eating animal fats as much as possible, any chef, from Grandma to Charlie Trotter, knows that a little bit of fat can mean a whole lot of flavor.

Season:

For carnivores, the season is always right for a slice of bacon, a juicy hamburger, or a thick steak. The month of January, just after New Year's resolutions are set, might be the one time of year that these stains are less likely to occur.

Areas of
Occurrence:

Lard and other animal fats don't migrate toward one particular staining area—any available surface is fair game. When tending the grill during summer barbecues, keep special attention focused on T-shirts and shorts, which all too easily fall prey to a renegade hot dog or Polish sausage. Diner employees and patrons run an especially high risk to their aprons, shirts, and dresses—diners are not called "greasy spoons" for no reason.

Time of Occurrence:	Animal fats never rest—with bacon at breakfast, deli sandwiches at lunch, pot roast at dinner, and pepperoni pizza as a midnight snack, a greasy animal-fat stain might appear at any time of the day or night. This stain is particularly tricky to detect in low lighting, and may escape notice until hours, days, or even months after the stain is acquired, especially if the clothing is retired to the closet after a night out and not washed immediately.

REMOVAL: *On fabric:*

1.   Use a dull knife or spoon to remove as much as possible.

 2.   Apply a laundry presoak (spot stain remover), and let stand for several minutes to allow it to penetrate fabric.

 3.   Rub liquid enzyme detergent into the stain and let stand several minutes, then launder in hottest water safe for fabric.

On wallpaper:

1.   Use a dull knife or spoon to remove as much as possible.

 2.   Place a sheet of absorbent paper, such as a paper towel or brown paper bag (ink side up), over the

stain and press with a warm iron. Replace the absorbent paper once saturated.

3. If the stain remains after pressing, make a paste of cornstarch or baking soda and water (at a ratio of approximately 3 to 1), and smear it on the stain.

4. Let the paste dry, then brush it off.

5. Repeat as necessary.

6. Apply a laundry presoak (spot stain remover) and let stand several minutes.

7. Wipe off with a damp cloth.

8. Repeat as necessary.

On carpet:

1. Sprinkle with an absorbent powder such as baking soda or talcum powder. Let stand several hours.

2. Vacuum.

3. If the stain remains, shampoo with a liquid carpet detergent according to manufacturer's directions. Or sprinkle with dry carpet-cleaning powder, let stand several hours, then vacuum.

20.   **HUMMUS**

General
Description:

A Middle Eastern sauce made from mashed chickpeas seasoned with lemon juice, garlic, and olive or sesame oil; usually served as a dip. Chickpeas (also known as garbanzo beans), the primary ingredient in hummus, were believed by the Romans to be a powerful aphrodisiac, leading the people to feed them to their stallions. A staple in Middle Eastern cuisines, hummus has gained tremendous popularity in the West as a dip for vegetables and breads, especially in communes and in urban areas with natural-food grocery stores.

Areas of
Occurrence:

Making generalizations regarding the trajectory of hummus is difficult due to its varying consistencies. If it has a runny texture (a high proportion of tahini and oil), its stain might appear on the fronts of sweaters, shirts, T-shirts, or blouses, as well as on the lap areas of pants. If the hummus is thick (mostly mashed chickpeas), you run less risk from its dripping and more from your sitting on a plate of hummus and vegetables at a party or a barbecue where hors d'oeuvres are served.

Variations of
Significance:

Falafel; sandwiches; wraps

REMOVAL: I.   **Use a dull knife or spoon to remove as much as possible.**

2. **Apply a laundry presoak (spot stain remover), and let stand for several minutes.**

3. **Rub liquid enzyme detergent into the stain and let stand several minutes.**

4. **Launder in the hottest water safe for the fabric.**

---

21. **PEANUT BUTTER**

General
Description:

A paste made from ground roasted peanuts, vegetable oil, sugar, and salt; available in smooth and chunky styles, as well as natural, which contains no added sugar, oil, or salt. For those who aren't allergic to nuts, peanut butter is a food that often inspires a wave of nostalgia. Ever since it was introduced to an ecstatic crowd at the Universal Exposition in 1904, peanut butter has been all the rage, with kids and adults alike. There are approximately 60,000 card-carrying members of the Adult Peanut Butter Lovers fan club in the United States and abroad, and after chocolate, peanuts and peanut butter are the second most popular ingredients in candy.

Season:

Peanut butter's popularity is at its peak while school is in session, but it is active year-round as a flavoring for desserts and as a topping on toast at breakfast time.

Areas of
Occurrence:

Walls, furniture, carpets, socks, shoes, pants, shirts, dresses, hats—there is no limit to the areas that might be affected by a peanut butter stain, especially when a young child is involved.

Time of
Occurrence:

Peanut butter is a food that can be served morning, noon, and night, but stainings are most probable between 11:30 A.M. and 1:00 P.M. in a grade-school cafeteria.

Variations of
Significance:

Cookies; ice cream; peanut butter and banana sandwiches; peanut butter and jelly sandwiches; peanut butter and marshmallow sandwiches; pies

REMOVAL:

1. Use a dull knife or spoon to remove as much as possible.

2. Apply a laundry presoak (spot stain remover) and let stand for several minutes to allow it to penetrate fabric.

3. Rub liquid enzyme detergent into the stain and let stand several minutes.

4. Launder in the hottest water safe for the fabric.

22.   **TUNA FISH**

General
Description:

Any of several large food and game fishes of the family Scombridae, including the albacore, bluefin, and yellowfin. Tuna is one of the few types of fish that may be more popular canned than fresh; fresh tuna have skin that is inedible. These fish swim at a steady rate of nine miles per hour for an indefinite period of time— they never stop moving, for they need continuous flow of water across their gills to breathe. It is estimated that a 15-year-old tuna travels one million miles in its lifetime.

Season:

Due to the popularity of canned tuna, this stain may appear in any season. From sandwich filling (when mixed with mayonnaise, pickles, onions, and celery) to salad complement to the sometimes-dreaded dinner staple tuna casserole, tuna will stain perennially. (See OIL, COOKING AND VEGETABLE on page 86; MAYONNAISE on page 82.)

Areas of
Occurrence:

Tuna is one stain that won't usually travel very far, as it is rarely runny or capable of being splattered. You will usually encounter a tuna stain on the fronts of trousers, shorts, dresses, jackets, and sweaters.

Time of
Occurrence:

A tuna stain will hardly ever occur in the morning, as there is little chance of it being used in omelets or as a cereal topping. This fish is not a particularly popular midnight snack, either, and so afternoon and evening are the most likely times for a tuna stain to develop.

Variations of
Significance:

Salad Nicoise; tuna casserole; tuna salad

REMOVAL: 1.   Use a dull knife or spoon to remove as much as possible.

2.   Rinse the back of the stain well with cold water.

3.   Apply a laundry presoak (spot stain remover) and let stand several minutes.

4.   Rub with a liquid enzyme detergent.

5.   Launder according to garment label.

Dairy Products

23.   **BABY FORMULA**

General
Description:
A special nutritive mixture, especially of milk or milk substitute with other ingredients in prescribed proportions, for feeding a baby. Formula was invented in 1867 by Henri Nestlé for mothers who were unable to breast-feed their babies. Since then, it has become widely useful for children who are allergic to milk and milk products, as well as for women who cannot breast-feed.

Season:

Since a baby may rely on formula from birth well into the first year, a formula stain can appear in any season. Babies might spit up more during the winter months, if they experience those particularly dreadful infant colds, thus these stains could be more common in winter.

Areas of
Occurrence:

This stain is undoubtedly most often found on the shoulders of all types of clothing. This includes both the front and the back of this part of a garment, as the most popular burping position for baby is over the shoulder. Though the most common, it is by no means the only place your garments might suffer them; babies are not choosy about where they spit up, so this stain may show up anywhere, from lapels to socks.

Time of   Any time you feed your baby is a time this stain can
Occurrence: appear.

REMOVAL: 1.   For fresh stains, soak and agitate the fabric
thoroughly in cold water. For dried stains, soak
fabric in a sudsy mixture of cold water and liquid
enzyme detergent up to 30 minutes, until the stain
is loosened.

    2.   Rinse well.

3.   If the stain remains, rub a liquid enzyme detergent
into the stain and let stand several minutes.

    4.   Launder according to garment label.

5.   If the stain remains, make a paste of unseasoned
meat tenderizer and water (at a ratio of approximately 3 to 1) and rub onto the stain.

6.   Let paste dry, then brush it off and rinse the fabric
well. If meat tenderizer is not available, soak the
stain in enzyme detergent and cold water mixture
for up to 30 minutes.

    7.   Apply a laundry presoak (spot stain remover) and
launder again. On white fabrics, bleach any
remaining stain by blotting with lemon juice and
setting it to dry in the sunlight.

24. **BUTTER OR MARGARINE**

General
Description:

Butter: *A fatty substance produced by agitating or churning cream; used as a cooking medium, ingredient, and topping.* Margarine: *A butter substitute made from animal or vegetable fats, or a combination of such fats mixed with flavorings, colorings, emulsifiers, preservatives, and vitamins and firmed through hydrogenation.* Butter and margarine are ubiquitous—either is used in just about every prepared food on the market. They are also found in almost every ingredient list in every cookbook in circulation.

Season:

Whether poured on popcorn, spread on holiday baked goods, or slathered on corn on the cob, butter and margarine cannot be escaped at any time of year.

Areas of
Occurrence:

Butter and margarine are tricky, and can stain unsuspecting victims almost anywhere. Remember to get extra napkins at the movie theater, or the lap area of your pants will be in grave danger. Melted butter can drip from popcorn, crab legs, baked potatoes, and corn on the cob. And be sure to look up when visiting high school cafeterias; pats of butter or margarine are a favorite weapon of rebellious students, who launch them at the ceiling in hopes that the pats will stick long enough to drop onto another student or an adult unaware of their pranks.

Variations of Significance: Corn on the cob; popcorn; seafood; toast

REMOVAL: *On fabric:*

1. Use a dull knife or spoon to remove as much as possible.

 2. Apply a laundry presoak (spot stain remover) and let stand for several minutes to allow it to penetrate fabric.

3. Rub liquid enzyme detergent into the stain and let stand several minutes.

 4. Launder in the hottest water safe for the fabric.

On carpet:

 1. Sprinkle with an absorbent powder such as baking soda or talcum powder. Let stand several hours.

 2. Vacuum. Repeat until you have removed as much stain as possible.

 3. If the stain remains, shampoo with a liquid carpet detergent according to manufacturer's directions. Or sprinkle with dry carpet-cleaning powder, let stand several hours, and then vacuum.

25. **CHEESE**

General
Description:

A food prepared from the curds of milk separated from the whey, often pressed and allowed to ripen. The variety of cheese is rivaled only by the uses for it, which are countless. This calcium-rich food is also quite good for you (in moderation, as with all things). Cheese helps strengthen bones to prevent osteoporosis, and helps to prevent tooth decay. Firm cheeses, like cheddar, are most effective for these purposes. To receive the most beneficial results, eat cheese alone or just after a meal.

Season:

Since the uses for cheese are so varied, the time of year this stain will occur is limited only by your own culinary imagination. Comfort foods mainly consisting of melted cheeses, like lasagna and grilled-cheese sandwiches, might be more common in winter. However, cheese is ever present at barbecues in the summer, so there may be no time of year you are safe from this stain.

Areas of
Occurrence:

Cheese is most likely to stain when melted—because of its consistency and tendency to plop in this state, laps of jeans and skirts are most susceptible. Stringy mozzarella leaves spots on the fronts and sleeves of turtlenecks and T-shirts alike. Given the popularity of omelets for breakfast, as well as grogginess in early morning, chef and diner can stain a nightgown or pair of pajamas with ease.

Time of Occurrence:	Late nights and early mornings are popular times to incur this stain, as defenses against it are down due to sleepiness. Also, you're likely to find this stain any time Italian or Mexican food is present.

Variations of Significance:	Baked ziti; blintzes; burritos; cannoli; cheesecake; cheesesteaks; enchiladas; grilled sandwiches; lasagna; macaroni and cheese; manicotti; nacho dip; omelets; pizza; quesadillas; quiche; soufflés; tacos

REMOVAL: *For fresh stains on fabric:*

1. Treat the stain as soon as possible. Soak and agitate fabric in cold water to loosen the stain, or sponge it with club soda.

2. If the stain remains, rub the stain with a liquid enzyme detergent and soak in tepid water for up to 30 minutes or until the stain is removed. Rub the stain lightly during soaking.

3. If the stain remains, apply a laundry presoak (spot stain remover) and let stand several minutes.

4. Launder according to garment label.

5. If a color stain remains, repeat steps 2 through 4.

For dried stains on fabric:

1. Use a dull knife or spoon to remove as much as possible.

2. Rub the stain with a liquid enzyme detergent and soak the garment in cold water for several hours or until the stain is removed. Rub the stain lightly during soaking.

3. See steps 3 through 5 for fresh stains.

26. **ICE CREAM**

General Description:
A rich frozen dessert made with dairy products, sugar, eggs, and various flavorings. After more than a century as a dessert for royalty alone, ice cream was made available to the general public for the first time at Café Procope, the first café in Paris, in 1670. With the advancement of technology, ice cream has ranked among the favorite desserts of children and adults the world over, as evidenced by the astounding variety of forms and flavors in which it is produced and sold. The ice-cream stain is influenced by the ingredients that are added to it; for instance, vanilla ice cream stains much differently than rocky road does. Therefore, some cross-referencing in this book may be necessary to effectively treat the stain at hand. (See Chocolate on page 71, Fruits or Berries on page 17.)

Season: Ice cream is a favorite summertime treat, so the proba-

bility of procuring this stain during the hottest months
of the year is nearly one hundred percent. However,
because ice cream is also a staple on many people's
dessert and/or comfort-food menus, this stain occurs
during any time of year.

Areas of   Ice-cream stains are nearly impossible to avoid due to
Occurrence: the treat's ephemeral frozenness. The range of this stain
is mind-boggling; ice cream can appear as far from the

mouth as the socks or the shoes when walking while
eating (especially due to faulty sugar-cone design). Be
especially on guard against the "rolling stain," which
occurs when a whole scoop of ice cream falls from the
top of your cone and rolls down the entire length of the
front of your shirt and/or shorts.

Variations of   Ice-cream cakes; milk shakes
Significance:

REMOVAL: *For fresh stains on fabric:*

1. **Treat the stain as soon as possible. Soak and agitate
fabric in cold water to loosen the stain, or sponge
it with club soda.**

2. **If the stain remains, rub it with a liquid enzyme
detergent and soak in tepid water for up to 30
minutes or until the stain is removed. Rub the**

stain lightly during soaking.

3. If the stain remains, apply a laundry presoak (spot stain remover) and let stand several minutes.

4. Launder according to garment label.

5. If a color stain remains, repeat steps 2 through 4.

6. If a grease stain remains, place the stain facedown on an absorbent cloth and treat with dry-cleaning fluid according to manufacturer's directions.

For dried stains on fabric:

1. Use a dull knife or spoon to remove as much as possible.

2. Rub the stain with a liquid enzyme detergent and soak the garment in cold water for several hours or until the stain is removed. Occasionally rub the stain between your thumbs during soaking.

3. See steps 3 through 6 for fresh stains, above.

27.   **MILK OR CREAM**

General
Description:

Milk: *An opaque white or bluish-white liquid secreted by the mammary glands of female mammals, serving as the nourishment for their young.* Cream: *The fatty part of milk that rises to the surface when the liquid is allowed to stand and is not homogenized.* Both milk and cream are instrumental in dessert baking and are considered a necessity by some coffee-drinkers. You would be hard-pressed to find any dessert recipe that does not use one of the two, and babies who aren't allergic live on the stuff.

Season:

Both coffee and baked goods are year-round goodies, and so milk or cream may find its way onto garments almost any time. The heavy baking months, during winter, are the most common times for this stain to occur.

Areas of
Occurrence:

Since milk and cream are almost always found in liquid form—and when they aren't, they won't likely stain—they tend to splash on sleeves and fronts of jackets and ties, especially in the early-morning rush to get coffee or cereal into your mouth. Additionally, since both of these dairy substances are highly spillable, shoes, socks, and pants are not immune to this stain.

Time of
Occurrence:

Early morning is undoubtedly the time this stain is most often encountered. Since almost all breakfast foods include milk or cream, and given that breakfast is often a hurried affair, this is the time they will most frequently splash or drip onto your clothing.

Variations of Significance:

Cereal; coffee; cream soups; creamed vegetables; egg dishes; fettuccine Alfredo

REMOVAL:

For fresh stains on fabric:

1. Treat the stain as soon as possible. Soak and agitate fabric in cold water to loosen the stain, or sponge it with club soda.

2. If the stain remains, rub the stain with a liquid enzyme detergent and soak in tepid water for up to 30 minutes or until the stain is removed. Rub the stain lightly during soaking.

3. If the stain remains, apply a laundry presoak (spot stain remover) and let stand several minutes.

4. Launder according to garment label.

5. If a color stain remains, repeat steps 2 through 4.

For dried stains on fabric:

1. Use a dull knife or spoon to remove as much as possible.

2. Rub the stain with a liquid enzyme detergent and soak the garment in cold water for several hours or until the stain is removed. Occasionally rub the stain between your thumbs while soaking.

3. See steps 3 through 5 for fresh stains, above.

---

28. **PUDDING**

General Description:
A soft, creamy, cooked dessert made with eggs, milk, sugar, and flavorings and thickened with flour or another starch. It is standard fare in the cafeterias of institutions like hospitals, schools, and nursing homes, as well on the menus of diners and some restaurants (especially those with salad bars). It can be found in a wide variety of flavors; some favorites are tapioca, chocolate, vanilla, pistachio, and butterscotch. Pudding is often used as filling for pies, donuts, and other baked goods, and has even held the distinction as actor Bill Cosby's favorite frozen treat, a "pudding pop."

Season:
Most pudding is consumed when institutional cafeterias are at their peak of activity. Pudding is most prevalent during the school year, when school cafeterias strive to feed young minds.

Areas of Occurrence:
The items that pudding stains affect are influenced by the location in which the stain is acquired. If in a hospital, sheets, blankets, and hospital gowns are prime tar-

gets; if in a school cafeteria, the possibilities are endless due to the potential for food fights. In the case of a food fight, all articles of clothing are at risk, in every area.

Time of
Occurrence:
Pay special attention during the hours of 11:00 A.M. to 1:00 P.M., as pudding is a dessert most often served with lunch.

Variations of
Significance:
Custards; pies; pudding pops

REMOVAL: *For fresh stains on fabric:*

1. Treat the stain as soon as possible. Soak and agitate fabric in cold water to loosen the stain, or sponge it with club soda.

2. If the stain remains, rub the stain with a liquid enzyme detergent and soak in tepid water for up to 30 minutes or until the stain is removed. Rub the stain lightly during soaking.

3. If the stain remains, apply a laundry presoak (spot stain remover) and let stand several minutes.

4. Launder according to garment label.

5. If a color stain remains, repeat steps 2 through 4.

For dried stains on fabric:

1. Use a dull knife or spoon to remove as much as possible.

2. Rub the stain with a liquid enzyme detergent and soak the garment in cold water for several hours or until the stain is removed. Rub the stain lightly during soaking.

3. See steps 3 through 5 for fresh stains, above.

---

29.   **SOUR CREAM**

General
Description:
Cream soured by the lactic acid produced by a ferment. Though sour cream may once have been simply a dip for chips or a baked-potato topping, it has lately experienced increased recognition due to the rise in popularity of Mexican food. It's no wonder plain old sour cream is so popular as an accompaniment to hot, spicy food—it soothes the taste buds. It—and other dairy products such as milk and yogurt—contains a protein that relieves the "burning."

Season:
Summer is a popular time for Mexican favorites like tacos, nachos, and burritos, but the stain that sour cream leaves is not confined to the warmer months. Since the baked potato is one of the world's favorite

comfort foods, and since sour cream is still the most popular topping for one, winter months will see this stain as well.

Areas of Occurrence:
Sour cream is particularly plop prone; it can fall anywhere from the butterfly collar of your favorite vintage shirt to the ends of your nylon-blend bell-bottoms.

Variations of Significance:
Baked potatoes; burritos; chili; chip dips; nachos; quesadillas; tacos

REMOVAL: *For fresh stains on fabric:*

1. Treat the stain as soon as possible. Soak and agitate fabric in cold water to loosen the stain, or sponge it with club soda.

2. If the stain remains, rub the stain with a liquid enzyme detergent and soak in tepid water for up to 30 minutes or until the stain is removed. Rub the stain lightly during soaking.

3. If the stain remains, apply a laundry presoak (spot stain remover) and let stand several minutes.

4. Launder according to garment label.

5. If a color stain remains, repeat steps 2 through 4.

For dried stains on fabric:

1. Use a dull knife or spoon to remove as much as possible.

2. Rub the stain with a liquid enzyme detergent and soak in cold water for several hours or until the stain is removed. Rub the stain lightly during soaking.

3. See steps 3 through 5 for fresh stains.

30.   **YOGURT**

General Description:
A thick, tart, custardlike fermented dairy product made from cow's milk to which bacteria cultures have been added. Yogurt has achieved an astounding popularity among the health-and-fitness conscious. When Dannon started selling yogurt with strawberries at the bottom in 1947, Americans joined Europeans as fans of this now-ubiquitous dairy product. Yogurt stains come in a variety of colors and consistencies, depending upon whether fruits or other flavorings have been added. Good not only for a light lunch or healthy snack, yogurt with live cultures may help prevent some digestive-tract problems and yeast infections.

Season: 	Yogurt stains are evergreen, though there is a notable increase in occurrence during the month of January, when millions of dieters are holding true to their New Year's resolution to eat healthier and lose weight.
Areas of Occurrence:	Commonly seen on clothes associated with the gym or working out, yogurt stains are also found on the fronts of shirts and blouses, and the lap areas of pants.
Time of Occurrence:	Yogurt stains usually occur when willpower is high—early morning, lunchtime, and even in the late afternoon before dinner. Chances of a yogurt stain in the evening or late night are slim, unless the offending substance is of the frozen variety.
Variations of Significance:	Frozen yogurt; yogurt-covered peanuts or raisins; yogurt drinks

REMOVAL: *For fresh stains on fabric:*

1. Use a dull knife or spoon to remove as much as possible.

2. Rinse the back of the stain with cold water. Soak and agitate the fabric in cold water to loosen the stain, or sponge it with club soda.

3. If the stain remains, rub with a liquid enzyme detergent and soak in tepid water for up to 30

minutes or until it is removed. Rub the stain lightly during soaking.

4. If the stain remains, apply a laundry presoak (spot
    stain remover) and let stand several minutes.

5. Launder according to garment label.

6. If a color stain remains, repeat steps 2 through 5.

For dried stains on fabric:

1. Use a dull knife or spoon to remove as much as
    possible.

2. Rub the stain with a liquid enzyme detergent and
    soak the garment in cold water for several hours, or
    until the stain is removed. Occasionally rub the
    stain between your thumbs during soaking.

3. See steps 4 through 6 for fresh stains, above.

Sauces and Condiments

31. 📷   **BARBECUE OR STEAK SAUCES**

General
Description:

A piquant sauce typically of vinegar, tomatoes, sugar, and spices, used for basting meats, poultry, and vegetables to be cooked over an open flame or broiled. Barbecue or steak sauces can be brushed on food just before cooking or barbecuing, or can be used as marinades.

Season:
☀

Barbecue sauce is most likely to stain clothing during the summer, when cookouts are par for the course. Steak sauce, however, can stain throughout the year, as both home cooking and fine dining involve T-bones or sirloins that may call for a little spicing up.

Areas of
Occurrence:

Your "KISS THE COOK" apron is a prime candidate for a barbecue-sauce stain, since only a fool would cook on the grill without some protection. Bathing suits, shorts, and T-shirts are likely victims as well. Steak sauce could stain your gown, fur coat, or tuxedo, depending on the fanciness of your favorite restaurant, or the fare at a gala or benefit.

Time of
Occurrence:

Summer barbecues are popular among family and friends. These can last well into the wee hours of the night, depending on whether tiki torches are involved. Any time from dusk until dawn is a fine time for a saucy stain of this sort.

REMOVAL: 1. Use a dull knife or spoon to remove as much as possible.

2. Flush the back of the stain immediately with cold water to force stain through the fabric.

3. Rub a liquid enzyme detergent into the stain and let stand several minutes. Occasionally rub the stain between your thumbs during soaking.

4. Rinse well.

5. Sponge with a mild bleach, such as white vinegar, hydrogen peroxide, or lemon juice, then rinse well.

6. Repeat steps 3 through 4 until no more stain can be removed.

7. Apply a laundry presoak (spot stain remover) and let stand several minutes.

8. Launder with an enzyme detergent.

9. Let garment dry in the sun for added bleaching.

10. If the stain remains, rub an enzyme detergent into it and then soak the garment in warm water for up to 30 minutes or until the stain is removed.

11. Rinse well.

 12. Apply laundry presoak (spot stain remover) and relaunder.

---

32. **CARAMEL**

General
Description:

A substance produced by cooking sugar until it becomes a thick, dark liquid; its color ranges from golden to dark brown. Caramel is a popular flavoring for food of all kinds, including desserts, candies, and sweet and savory sauces. Although "butterscotch" and "caramel" are sometimes used interchangeably, butterscotch is distinguished by the absence of milk or milk substitutes from its recipe. Both are obtained by boiling sugar to or beyond 240 degrees Fahrenheit.

Season:

Caramel is a favorite of holiday bakers and ice-cream-sundae makers alike; therefore you are just as likely to run into this stain during the December holidays as in the heat of summer vacation. There is, however, always a chance of getting this stain when visiting the candy-bar section at the local convenience store any time of year.

Areas of
Occurrence:

Caramel is a stringy substance, and it rarely stains as a single blob like most sauces and condiments do. This is a stain that might run from the front of your shirt to your arm, or vice versa.

Time of
Occurrence: Caramel stains are telltale evidence of your weakest
                moments—the late-night craving, the post-breakup ice-
                cream sundae, the candy bar just before dinner.

Variations of   Candy bars; ice-cream sundaes
Significance:

REMOVAL: *For fresh stains on fabric:*

1.   Use a dull knife or spoon to remove as much as
     possible.

2.   Rinse well with cold water.

3.   Rub liquid laundry detergent into the stain and
     let stand several minutes.

4.   Rinse well in hot water, letting the water pass
     quickly through the fabric.

5.   If the stain remains, stretch the stained fabric over
     a basin. Boil three or more cups of water in a pot
     or teakettle and pour over the stain from a height
     of 1 to 2 feet. (This may require two people: one
     to hold the fabric taut and the other to pour the
     water.) This procedure will force the stain through
     the fabric.

6.   If the stain remains, apply a laundry presoak

(spot stain remover) and launder according to garment label.

For dried stains on fabric:

1. Rub liquid laundry detergent into stain.

2. Soak garment in a soapy mixture of detergent and cold water for up to 30 minutes to loosen the stain. Agitate stain while soaking.

3. See steps 3 through 6 for fresh stains, above.

---

33. **CHOCOLATE**

General Description:

A candy or beverage made from fermented, roasted, and ground cacao seeds, often sweetened. In its nearly three-thousand-year-old history, chocolate has been more than just a popular dessert or snack—it has served as medicinal tonic, religious symbol, currency, and even aphrodisiac. Today 600,000 tons of chocolate are consumed in the world each year. It is found in many forms, including powder, syrup, solid bars, molded woodland animals and popular cultural icons, and as flavoring for cakes, pastries, frostings, cookies, ice creams, puddings, custards, drinks, and other desserts, and even some hearty entrees, like chicken mole.

Season: A chocolate stain can appear in any season but is espe-

            cially prevalent near holidays—particularly Christmas,
            Halloween, and Easter—as well as at times of celebra-
            tion where dessert is likely to be served. Chocolate ice
            cream is almost certainly found more often on summer
            clothing, like tank tops and shorts, and cocoa is more
            prevalent during the cold winter months. There is an
            increased chance of chocolate stains during "break-up
            season," year-round.

Areas of   Chocolate stains are found on the fronts of blouses and
Occurrence: shirts, but aren't confined to those spots. Ice cream can

            travel as far as the pants, skirt, or shoes (see Ice Cream on
            page 55). Bakers, pastry chefs, waiters, and waitresses may
            run the risk of this stain every moment they're on the job.

Time of   Chocolate stains will likely appear at dessert time. In
Occurrence: some cases, they occur in the wee hours of a particularly
            trying night. You might not notice the stain at this time,
            as it would likely occur in a darkened room, with only
            the glow of the television as your light-source.

Variations of   Chocolate chip cookies; chocolate-covered fruit;
Significance: milk shakes; mole sauce

REMOVAL: 1. **Use a dull knife or spoon to remove as much as
                    possible.**

                2. **Rinse the back of the stain well with cold water.**

3. Rub a liquid enzyme detergent into the stain, then soak it in cold water for 30 minutes or until the stain is loosened. Old, persistent stains may need to be soaked for several hours. Occasionally rub the stain between your thumbs as it soaks.

4. Rinse well and allow to dry.

5. If a grease stain remains, apply a laundry presoak (spot stain remover) or treat with dry-cleaning fluid according to manufacturer's directions.

6. Launder according to garment label.

34. **GRAVY**

General Description:

The fat and juices of cooked foods, often diluted with water, milk, wine, or stock, and thickened with flour or cornstarch; used as a sauce. Gravy is generally known as a "reduction sauce," and can be made from the juices of many types of cooked food, from meat to vegetables. It's easy to make—though grocery stores generally carry it in cans—and complements a variety of recipes nicely. There is some controversy as to whether lumps are desirable in gravy; some say the lumps add a homemade flavor, others prefer their gravy smooth. Whichever way you have it, though, it will still stain linens and clothing.

Season: Turkey season is gravy-stain season; that is,
           Thanksgiving and Christmastime see more of these
           stains. Because a heaping plate of meat, potatoes, and
           vegetables smothered with gravy is a hearty and com-
           forting meal, however, the occasional gravy stain may
           appear throughout winter and fall.

Areas of   Since gravy is a food with a tendency to splash and/or
Occurrence: splatter, this is a far-reaching stain. The sleeves of a wool
           sweater or the lap areas of pants and skirts receive this
           stain the most. Tablecloths and napkins are especially
           vulnerable, as gravy boats are notoriously bad at con-
           taining all the drips.

Time of   Dinnertime is the most common time to encounter this
Occurrence: stain. Though some eat their big holiday meals early in
           the day, at a time considered lunchtime, and some eat
           later, there's no telling when you'll find it. The only time
           of little risk might be early morning, when gravy is not a
           popular food.

Variations of Biscuits; chicken; french fries; pot roast; Salisbury steak;
Significance: turkey

REMOVAL: *On fabric:*

           1. **Use a dull knife or spoon to remove as much as
               possible.**

2. Blot the stain with a paper towel.

3. Mix a solution of 1 tablespoon liquid enzyme detergent to 1 cup of cold water. Soak the fabric in the solution for several hours.

4. Rinse well.

5. If the stain persists, rub a liquid enzyme detergent into the stain.

6. Launder with liquid enzyme detergent.

7. If the stain remains, repeat steps 3 through 6.

On carpet:

1. Use a dull knife or spoon to remove as much as possible.

2. Blot remaining liquid with an absorbent cloth.

3. Sponge the stain with a sudsy mixture of liquid enzyme detergent and cold water, then sponge with clear cold water. Repeat until you have removed as much stain as possible.

4. If the stain remains, sponge with a mild bleach, such as lemon juice or hydrogen peroxide (do not

let it saturate carpet), then sponge with clear cold water. Repeat as needed.

5. If the stain remains, treat with a carpet spotter according to manufacturer's directions.

---

35.   **HONEY**

General
Description:

A sweet, usually viscous, liquid made by bees from flower nectar and stored in the cells of their hives for food; consumed fresh or after processing, it is usually used as a nutritive sweetener. Honey is not easily produced—bees must collect nectar from about two million flowers to make a one-pound comb of honey. However, once honey has been created, it's not easily gotten rid of. It seems it is the only food that does not spoil. Honey found in the tombs of Egyptian pharaohs has been tasted by archeologists and found to be edible.

Season:

Honey is consumed year-round, but its stain is especially prevalent during the winter flu season, when honey-sweetened tea is just what the doctor orders.

Areas of
Occurrence:

Honey is a stringy substance, and it rarely stains as a single blob like most sauces and condiments do. This is a stain that might stretch from the front of your shirt to the back of your arm, or vice versa.

Time of Occurrence:	Honey stains are most likely to appear in the morning, around breakfast, when an errant piece of honey-covered toast or biscuit escapes grasp.

REMOVAL: *For fresh stains on fabric:*

1. Use a dull knife or spoon to remove as much as possible.

 2. Rinse well with cold water.

3. Rub liquid laundry detergent into the stain and let stand several minutes.

 4. Rinse well in hot water, letting the water pass quickly through the fabric.

 5. If the stain remains, stretch the stained fabric over a basin. Boil three or more cups of water in a pot or teakettle and pour over the stain from a height of 1 to 2 feet. (This may require two people: one to hold the fabric taut and the other to pour the water.) This procedure will force the stain through the fabric.

 6. If the stain remains, apply a laundry presoak (spot stain remover) and launder according to garment label.

For dried stains on fabric:

1. Rub liquid laundry detergent into stain. Soak garment in a soapy mixture of detergent and cold water for up to 30 minutes to loosen the stain. Agitate stain while soaking.

2. See steps 3 through 6 for fresh stains, above.

---

36. **KETCHUP**

General Description:

A condiment consisting of pureed tomatoes, onions, vinegar, sugar, and spices. Though the ingredients of ketchup don't usually differ from nation to nation, the primary uses for it do, for example, in Sweden, on pasta; Eastern Europe, on pizza; Japan, on rice; Denmark, on spaghetti; Thailand, as dip for potato chips; Great Britain, on fish and chips; Spain and India, on eggs; and in the United States, on hamburgers, hot dogs, and french fries.

Season:

While ketchup is unarguably the most popular condiment at a summer cookout, this won't be the only time and place you'll find this stain, since hamburgers and french fries are year-round foods. A ketchup stain could appear literally any time at all.

Areas of Occurrence:

This is a foodstuff with a tendency to plop and splatter. From the collar of your windbreaker after eating a hot

dog at the game, to the hem of your dress after the
church picnic, ketchup is found to be an equal-
opportunity stain.

REMOVAL: 1. Use a dull knife or spoon to remove as much as
possible.

2. Flush the back of the stain immediately with cold
water to force the stain through fabric.

3. Rub a liquid enzyme detergent into the stain and
let stand several minutes. Rub the fabric between
thumbs during soaking.

4. Rinse well.

5. Sponge with a mild bleach, such as white vinegar,
hydrogen peroxide, or lemon juice, then rinse well.

6. Repeat steps 3 through 5 until no more stain can
be removed.

7. Apply a laundry presoak (spot stain remover) and
let stand several minutes.

8. Launder with an enzyme detergent.

9. Let garment dry in the sun for added bleaching.

10. If the stain remains, rub an enzyme detergent into the stain and then soak garment in warm water for up to 30 minutes or until the stain is removed. Rinse well.

 11. Apply laundry presoak (spot stain remover) and relaunder.

---

37.   **MAPLE SYRUP**

General Description:

A reddish-brown, viscous liquid with a sweet, distinctive flavor, made by reducing the sap of the North American maple tree. Between 30 and 50 gallons of maple sap are evaporated to yield one gallon of syrup, making the sugar content of syrup 66.5 percent, while the sugar content of the sap is only about 2.5 percent. In the United States, Vermont is the largest producer of this sticky substance, which is served as a sauce with pancakes, waffles, and other breakfast fare.

Season:

As maple syrup is a favorite at breakfast tables year-round, this stain has potential unlimited by time.

Areas of Occurrence:

Maple-syrup stains appear most frequently on the fronts of shirts, blouses, jackets, and the lap areas of pants and dresses. Because maple syrup is most often consumed in the morning, as we struggle to regain our grasp of the world, pay close attention to the cuffs and elbows of sleeves; they are targets of this sticky stain when you are unaware.

Time of Occurrence:

Maple-syrup stains aren't only acquired in the morning, though maple syrup is used to enhance the foods served at breakfast. With the rise of the 24-hour diner, truck drivers, folks working the third shift, and many teenagers consume pancakes with maple syrup at all hours.

REMOVAL: *On fabric:*

1. Use a dull knife or spoon to remove as much as possible.

2. Rinse well with cold water.

3. Rub liquid laundry detergent into the stain. Let stand several minutes.

4. Rinse well in hot water, letting the water pass quickly through the fabric.

5. If the stain remains, stretch the stained fabric over a basin. Boil three or more cups of water in a pot or teakettle and pour over the stain from a height of 1 to 2 feet. (This may require two people: one to hold the fabric taut and the other to pour the water.) This procedure will force the stain through the fabric.

6. **If the stain remains, apply a laundry presoak (spot stain remover) and launder according to garment label.**

38. **MAYONNAISE**

General
Description:

A thick dressing of egg yolks, vinegar or lemon juice, oil, and seasonings. Mayonnaise is said to be the invention of the French chef employed by Duke de Richelieu in 1756. While the duke was defeating the British at Port Mahon, his chef was creating a victory feast that included a sauce made of cream and eggs. When the chef realized there was no cream in the kitchen, he improvised and substituted olive oil. The chef named it *mahonnaise* in honor of the duke's victory, and a new culinary delight was born. This condiment has since become a staple in kitchens around the globe.

Season:

Though mayonnaise is probably more commonly used as a condiment for summer picnic foods, like potato salad and pasta salad, a large contingent of the population enjoys egg-salad or tuna-salad sandwiches throughout the year. Because of its wide appeal as an accompaniment to various foods, mayonnaise stains clothing year-round.

Time of
Occurrence:

You'll rarely find a need for mayonnaise in the morning. This stain appears most often at lunchtime,

when a sandwich or french fries calls for a healthy
dollop of the stuff.

Variations of   Chicken salad; egg salad; ham salad; pasta salad; potato
Significance: salad; sandwiches; tuna salad

REMOVAL: *On fabric:*

1. Use a dull knife or spoon to remove as much as
   possible.

2. Apply a laundry presoak (spot stain remover). Let
   stand for several minutes.

3. Rub liquid enzyme detergent into the stain and let
   stand several minutes.

4. Launder in the hottest water safe for the fabric.

On carpet:

1. Sprinkle with an absorbent powder, such as baking
   soda or talcum powder. Let stand several hours.

2. Vacuum.

3. Repeat until you have removed as much stain as
   possible.

4. **If the stain remains, shampoo with a liquid carpet detergent according to manufacturer's directions. Or sprinkle with dry carpet-cleaning powder, let stand several hours, and vacuum.**

<hr>

39.   **MUSTARD**

General
Description:
A smooth, somewhat runny condiment made from white or yellow mustard seeds, sugar, vinegar, and turmeric, that has a mild, slightly sharp flavor and bright yellow color. Varieties of mustard include Chinese, English, German, and Dijon. Mustard is the second most popular condiment in the United States (ketchup being the first). It is standard fare on just about any fast-food hamburger or hot dog, as well as on many other popular snacks, such as soft pretzels.

Season:

Due to the ubiquitousness of fast food, mustard stains occur year-round. The popularity of backyard grills leads to an increase in the overall prevalence of mustard in spring and summer.

Areas of
Occurrence:

Mustard is a wily substance that will plop from unexpected places directly onto the fronts of shirts, dresses, pants, shorts, and skirts.

REMOVAL: *For fresh stains on fabric:*

1. Use a dull knife or spoon to remove as much as possible.

 2. Hold the stain upside down under a stream of cold water to force as much stain out of the fabric as possible.

3. Rub a liquid enzyme detergent into the stain (the stain may change color). Let stand several minutes.

4. Rinse well. Repeat until no more stain can be removed.

 5. Apply a laundry presoak (spot stain remover) and let stand several minutes.

 6. Launder with a liquid enzyme detergent.

7. If the stain remains, let garment dry in the sun, then repeat steps 3 through 6.

For dried stains on fabric:

1. Rub glycerin into the stain and let stand until loosened, up to 1 hour.

2. See steps 2 through 6 for fresh stains, above.

On carpet:

1. For fresh stains, use a dull knife or spoon to remove as much as possible. If the stain is dry, first rub glycerin into it and let stand until loosened, up to 1 hour, then scrape away as much as possible.

2. Blot the stain with a damp absorbent cloth.

3. If the stain remains, treat with a carpet spotter.

 4. Lighten any remaining color stain with a mild bleach, such as hydrogen peroxide, white vinegar, or lemon juice.

5. Blot with water.

---

40.   **OIL, COOKING OR VEGETABLE**

General
Description: *Any of a large class of substances typically unctuous, viscous, combustible, liquid at ordinary temperatures, and soluble in ether or alcohol but not in water.* The edible types of oils are made from such things as nuts, seeds, vegetables, legumes, and fruits. Though canola and vegetable oils are indispensable for everyday stovetop cooking, olive oil is quickly becoming the most popular oil in the u.s. kitchen, both for cooking and for flavoring. Historically, olive oil was used to light the candelabra in the ancient

Temple of Jerusalem, as far back as 164 B.C. Today during Hanukkah, the finest olive oil is still used to light oil lamps and to cook traditional holiday foods.

Season: Since these oils are used to cook everything from popcorn to stir-fry, oil stains are not limited to or more common in any particular season.

Areas of Occurrence: Oil splatters easily; it pops and sputters when it gets hot. Therefore, no part of your clothing is safe from the stuff, though sleeves of sweaters and blouses, not to mention the fronts of aprons, are most vulnerable during cooking. Of course, when a food cooked in oil falls on your jeans or the front of your jacket, a stain will appear just as easily.

Variations of Significance: Chicken dishes; Chinese food; deep-fried foods; pasta dishes; pasta salad

REMOVAL: *On fabric:*

1. Use a dull knife or spoon to remove as much as possible.

 2. Apply a laundry presoak (spot stain remover), and let stand for several minutes.

3. If the stain remains, rub liquid enzyme detergent into the stain and let stand several minutes.

4. Launder in the hottest water safe for the fabric.

On wallpaper:

1. Use a dull knife or spoon to remove as much as possible.

2. Place a sheet of absorbent paper, such as a paper towel or brown paper bag (ink side up), over the stain and press with a warm iron. Replace the absorbent paper once saturated.

3. If the stain remains after pressing, make a paste of cornstarch or baking soda and water (at a ratio of approximately 3 to 1) and smear it on the stain.

4. Let the paste dry, then brush it off. Repeat as necessary.

5. Apply a laundry presoak (spot stain remover) and let stand several minutes.

6. Wipe off with a damp cloth.

7. Repeat as necessary.

On carpet:

1. Sprinkle with an absorbent powder, such as baking

soda or talcum powder. Let stand several hours.

2. Vacuum. Repeat until you have removed as much stain as possible.

3. If the stain remains, shampoo with a liquid carpet detergent according to manufacturer's directions.

---

41. **RELISH**

General Description:
Cooked or pickled sauce usually made with vegetables or fruits and often used as a condiment; can be smooth or chunky, sweet or savory, and hot or mild. Relish is a standard condiment used at baseball parks, barbecues, and picnics—wherever there are grilled hot dogs, you are sure to find relish. According to the National Hot Dog and Sausage Council, chunky condiments like relish should be applied directly to the hot dog (not to the bun), just after wet condiments like mustard and chili but before spices, such as salt or pepper.

Season:
Relish stains occur primarily in summertime but are known to occur even during the coldest days of winter at football stadiums across the United States.

Areas of Occurrence:

In summer, stains are likely to be found on T-shirts and shorts; in winter, on the fronts of brightly colored jackets bearing football team logos.

REMOVAL:

1. Rinse the back of the stain immediately and thoroughly with cold water to neutralize the acid.

2. Place garment on an absorbent cloth and sponge well with ammonia, starting from the outside of the stain's edge. Replace cloth underneath as it becomes saturated. (If treating stains on wool or silk, dilute ammonia with an equal amount of cold water.) If ammonia is not available, substitute a baking-soda paste by mixing baking soda with water at a ratio of approximately 3 to 1. Rub paste into stain.

3. Rinse well.

4. Repeat as needed.

5. If a color stain remains, apply a laundry presoak (spot stain remover) and let stand several minutes.

6. Launder according to garment label.

---

42. **SALAD DRESSING, CREAMY**

General Description:

A sauce used on any type of salad, made from a base of mayonnaise with spices or vegetables added for flavor. French and Russian salad dressings do not exist in France and Russia. Although Russian dressing once contained a Russian ingredient (caviar), they both remain purely American concoctions. Popular varieties at salad bars include the aforementioned Russian and French, as well as ranch, bleu cheese (Roquefort), and creamy Parmesan.

Season:

Even though salads themselves are probably most popular during the summer months, creamy salad dressings are often used in baked dishes throughout the year, so their stains aren't limited to the warmest time of the year.

Areas of Occurrence:

This thick, liquidy substance tends to land on clothing in the lap areas, as well as on sleeves and fronts of garments.

Time of Occurrence:

Since salad dressing is primarily used to enhance salad, and salad is primarily served as a complete lunch or a side dish with dinner, afternoons and evenings are when you'll be most likely to encounter this stain.

Variations of Significance:

Baked ranch chicken; pasta dishes; salad; vegetable dip

REMOVAL:

1. **Use a dull knife or spoon to remove as much as possible.**

2. **Rub the stain with a liquid enzyme detergent and soak in cold water for up to 30 minutes or until the stain is removed. Rub the stain lightly between thumbs during soaking.**

3. If the stain remains, apply a laundry presoak (spot stain remover) and let stand several minutes.

4. Launder according to garment label.

5. If a color stain remains, repeat steps 2 through 4.

43. 📷 **SALAD DRESSING, VINAIGRETTE**

General Description:

An emulsion of oil and vinegar (usually three parts oil and one part vinegar) seasoned with herbs, spices, salt, and pepper. Known to some as Italian dressing and to others as French, vinaigrette is quite possibly the most popular salad dressing in western cultures. This dressing's stains are difficult to treat due to the difference in the consistency and makeup of the two main ingredients, oil and vinegar. (See VINEGAR on page 100; OIL, COOKING OR VEGETABLE on page 86.)

Season:

Vinaigrette stains are not particular to a season, though they may be more prevalent in warmer months when light lunches of lettuce and pasta salads are standard fare.

Areas of Occurrence:

A stray vinaigrette-covered vegetable from a salad or sandwich has a standard downward trajectory—therefore, vinaigrette stains are most common to the fronts of shirts, blouses, jackets, and to the lap areas of pants and dresses. Before shaking a bottle of vinaigrette, always be sure to check that the cap is tightly secured, or you may find yourself with stains anywhere on your body or anywhere in the room (especially on the walls).

REMOVAL:

1. Use a dull knife or spoon to remove as much as possible.

2. Apply a laundry presoak (spot stain remover) and let stand several minutes to allow it to penetrate fabric.

3. Rub liquid enzyme detergent into the stain and let stand several minutes.

4. Launder in the hottest water safe for the fabric.

---

44. **SALSA**

General Description:

Literally the Spanish word for "hot sauce," a cooked or fresh combination of fruits and/or vegetables. The most common salsa is the refreshing Latino mixture of tomatoes and chili peppers. Salsa has enjoyed an amazing rise in popularity in recent years due to its versatility and healthfulness; it goes with much more than just Mexican fare, and is generally fat-free. In fact, salsa ranks third among the most popular condiments in the United States today, surpassed only by ketchup and mustard.

Season:

Due to the aforementioned rise in popularity of Mexican food in general and salsa in particular, you may encounter salsa stains throughout the year.

Areas of
Occurrence:

Since margaritas often accompany Mexican dinners, there is virtually no limit to where you'll find salsa stains on clothing. Additionally, since salsa comprises both liquid and solid matter, it will run as well as plop, thus the fronts of dresses, trousers, and jackets are not safe from the salsa stain.

Time of
Occurrence:

Salsa may show up in breakfast foods, such as omelets; therefore, you might encounter this stain in the morning, though that will not be the norm. Afternoons and evenings are the times you are most likely to acquire this stain, though the amount of tequila you imbibe during the consumption of salsa could impair the process of detection until the next day or even later.

Variations of
Significance:

Mexican dishes; omelets

REMOVAL:

1. Use a dull knife or spoon to remove as much as possible.

2. Flush the back of the stain immediately with cold water to force the stain through fabric.

3. Rub a liquid enzyme detergent into the stain and

let stand several minutes. Occasionally rub the
stain between your thumbs during soaking.

4. Rinse well.

 5. Sponge with a mild bleach, such as white vinegar,
hydrogen peroxide, or lemon juice, then rinse well.

6. Repeat steps 3 through 5 until no more stain can
be removed.

 7. Apply a laundry presoak (spot stain remover) and
let stand several minutes.

8. Launder with an enzyme detergent. Let garment
dry in the sun for added bleaching.

9. If the stain remains, rub an enzyme detergent into
the stain and then soak garment in warm water for
up to 30 minutes or until the stain is gone.

 10. Rinse well.

 11. Apply laundry presoak (spot stain remover) and
relaunder.

45. **SOY SAUCE**

General
Description:
A sauce made from fermented boiled soybeans and roasted wheat or barley; its color ranges from light to dark brown and its flavor is generally rich and salty. Soy sauce is a staple condiment of Asian cuisine; it can be found in many forms, including small packages with Chinese or Japanese take-out, in little pitchers on the tables of Chinese and Japanese restaurants, or in bottles for sale at supermarkets.

Areas of
Occurrence:

Soy-sauce stains are difficult to avoid when opening those small packets that are included with Chinese or Japanese take-out. Even when opened with extreme care, these little packets often spray all over the place, staining not only the sleeves and fronts of blouses, shirts, and dresses but trousers, shorts, skirts, and tablecloths, upholstered furniture, rugs, and carpets. These areas can also be affected when a novice attempts to use chopsticks. An errant dumpling will inevitably land in the dish of soy sauce, splattering the contents.

Time of
Occurrence:
Soy-sauce stains typically occur at times not commonly thought of as mealtimes, such as when you are running behind schedule and want a quick bite to eat before an engagement to which it is important to be punctual.

REMOVAL: *For fresh stains on fabric:*

1. Force cold water through the back of the stain.

2. Rinse well.

3. If the stain remains, apply a laundry presoak (spot stain remover) and let stand several minutes.

4. Launder according to garment label.

For dried stains on fabric:

1. Force cold water through the back of the stain.

2. Rinse well.

3. Rub liquid laundry detergent into the stain and let stand several minutes. Rub the stain between your thumbs as you rinse it in cold water. Repeat until you have removed as much stain as possible.

4. If the stain remains, rub with liquid laundry detergent and soak in lukewarm water, agitating often, for up to 30 minutes or until the stain is removed.

5. Rinse well.

6. See steps 3 and 4 for fresh stains, above.

46.   **TOMATO SAUCE**

General
Description:

A mixture of tomatoes, vegetables, and spices, pureed or stirred together to make a sauce that can be thin or chunky in consistency and that is used to accent pastas and a variety of other foods. Though tomato sauce may seem quintessentially Italian, tomatoes were actually introduced to Italy by the Americas.

Season:

Since there are so many different varieties of tomato sauce, and since the uses for tomato sauce are so diverse, stains from the stuff know no season.

Areas of
Occurrence:

Your apron and sleeves will bear the brunt of this stain as you concoct your favorite tomato sauce, since it tends to pop and sputter as it simmers. While eating the delicious mixture, you'll find that no matter how thick or chunky with vegetables it is, it is a liquid that will splatter quite easily, so watch pant legs, collars, and sweaters for telltale signs of the Italian meal well-enjoyed.

Time of
Occurrence:

Evening will most certainly be the time when this stain occurs. The dimness of most good Italian restaurants and the copious red wine that accompanies Italian meals might make detection an event for the next day. (See WINE, RED on page 119.)

Variations of
Significance:

Eggplant, chicken, or veal Parmesan; lasagna; manicotti; pizza; spaghetti

REMOVAL: 1. Use a dull knife or spoon to remove as much as possible.

2. Flush the back of the stain immediately with cold water to force the stain through fabric.

3. Rub a liquid enzyme detergent into the stain and let stand several minutes. Rub the fabric between thumbs.

4. Rinse well.

5. Sponge with a mild bleach, such as white vinegar, hydrogen peroxide, or lemon juice, then rinse well.

6. Repeat steps 3 through 5 until no more stain can be removed.

7. Apply a laundry presoak (spot stain remover) and let stand several minutes.

8. Launder with an enzyme detergent.

9. Let garment dry in the sun for added bleaching.

10. If the stain remains, rub an enzyme detergent into the stain and then soak garment in warm water for up to 30 minutes or until the stain is gone.

11. Rinse well.

12. Apply laundry presoak (spot stain remover) and relaunder.

---

47. **VINEGAR**

General Description:

From the French vin aigre *(sour wine), a weak solution of acetic acid made from a fermented liquid such as cider, wine, champagne, or beer, subjected to certain bacterial activity; generally clear, the liquid can be tinted various shades, depending on the base liquid.* Strong enough to melt pearls, vinegar was the most potent acid known to the ancients. It is now most likely found as an ingredient in marinades or salad dressings, though it can also accompany salty foods like potato chips and french fries.

Season:

Vinegar stains occur at all times of year. However, you must have a heightened awareness of the potential for vinegar stains during spring, summer, and early fall, when vendors at fairs, amusement parks, and ball parks sell french fries seasoned with vinegar in leaky paper cups and cones.

Areas of Occurrence:

This stain is most likely to be found on the fronts of jeans, shorts, blouses, dresses, jackets, and sweaters, but can sometimes reach as far as your shoes when vinegar is used as a condiment for french fries. When using vinegar to clean windows, be extra careful of sleeves.

Time of Occurrence:	The acidity of vinegar makes it an unlikely choice as an ingredient in breakfast foods, thus, vinegar stainings are most likely during the salad course of midday or evening meals or times of recreation.

Variations of Significance:	Condiment for french fries; glass cleaner; marinades for meat; vinaigrette

REMOVAL:

1. Rinse the back of the stain immediately and thoroughly with cold water to neutralize the acid.

2. Place garment on an absorbent cloth and sponge well with ammonia, starting from the outside of the stain's edge. Replace cloth underneath as it becomes saturated. (If treating stains on wool or silk, dilute ammonia with an equal amount of cold water.) If ammonia is not available, substitute a baking-soda paste, mixing baking soda and water at a ratio of approximately 3 to 1. Rub into stain.

3. Rinse well.

4. Repeat as needed.

5. If a color stain remains, apply a laundry presoak (spot stain remover) and let stand several minutes.

6. **Launder according to garment label.**

48. **WORCESTERSHIRE SAUCE**

General
Description:
A dark, spicy condiment usually made of soy sauce, vinegar, garlic, tamarind, onions, molasses, lime, anchovies, and other seasonings, originally bottled in Worcestershire, England. Though not as popular as its close cousin soy sauce, it is instrumental in seasoning foods, from meat, gravy, and soup to snack mixes and the drink Bloody Mary. Testament to its quiet but enduring popularity, Worcestershire sauce has been commercially available for more than 165 years—45 years longer than ketchup.

Season:

Because the sauce is most frequently used in heavier fare, such as meat, gravy, and hearty soups, a Worcestershire stain will most probably occur more in the colder months of the year.

Areas of
Occurrence:
Another of those liquid condiments that splatter easily, especially because of the bottle it so often comes in, this sauce will splash onto cuffs and collars, as well as the fronts of blouses and slacks.

Time of
Occurrence:
There is little call for this sauce in the morning, though a Bloody Mary is no stranger to the festive brunch. But this stain will most likely strike in the hours between dusk and dawn.

Variations of Significance:	Barbecue sauce; Bloody Mary; gravy; marinades; snack mixes; soups

REMOVAL:

1. Rinse the back of the stain immediately and thoroughly with cold water to neutralize the acid.

2. Place garment on an absorbent cloth and sponge well with ammonia, starting from the outside of the stain's edge. Replace cloth underneath as it becomes saturated. (If treating stains on wool or silk, dilute ammonia with an equal amount of cold water.) If ammonia is not available, substitute a baking-soda paste, mixing baking soda and water at the ratio of approximately 3 to 1. Rub paste into stain.

3. Rinse well.

4. Repeat as needed.

5. If a color stain remains, apply a laundry presoak (spot stain remover) and let stand several minutes.

6. Launder according to garment label.

Beverages

49.   **ALCOHOLIC BEVERAGES**

General
Description:

Any of a large number of drinks that contain a distilled alcoholic mixture of some kind, including vodka, gin, whiskey, and scotch, among others. Can be served with ice, combined with other potables (such as tonic water, juices, colas, or another alcoholic mixture), or served straight. Thought by some to be necessary for human survival, liquor has played a substantial role in human social affairs. So vital is alcohol to human history that a Chinese imperial edict circa 1116 B.C. claimed its use in moderation to be required by heaven. It is not uncommon to hear someone claim alcohol played an integral part in his or her marital status, financial affairs, or even coming-into-existence.

Season:

Alcoholic beverages often figure prominently in both times of celebration and times of trauma, thus their stains occur throughout the year. Many holidays and vacations involve consumption of alcohol, and these beverages often play a large role in human mating rituals. Before or during a "blind date," alcohol stains are likely to appear as jittery nerves begin to relax. Tax season is also a time of the year when you might run an increased risk of acquiring stains from alcoholic beverages.

Areas of
Occurrence:

These stains may appear anywhere on the fronts of
shirts and dresses, or be splashed on pant legs and skirts
as the hours grow later. The eventuality that another
person might accidentally knock his glass into your back
makes for stains that are noticeable to all but yourself.

Time of
Occurrence:

Alcohol stains belong to that class for which the time of
acquisition and the time of discovery are very different.
Stainings are most likely during the evening and late-
night hours, when parties, celebrations, and bar-happen-
ings take place. Society dictates that you not obtain a
stain from an alcoholic beverage before 10 A.M. You are
likely to *find* a stain in the morning when reviewing the
previous night's activities. Realizing the acquisition of a
stain while consuming alcoholic beverages is unlikely,
unless the staining occurs before intoxication sets in.

REMOVAL:

1. Rinse back of stain well with cold water or club soda.

2. If the stain remains, rub with dishwashing liquid
    or liquid enzyme detergent. Let stand several min-
    utes. (Do not use bar or natural soap of any kind
    or the stain will set.)

3. Rinse well with cold water.

4. Launder according to garment label.

5. If the stain remains, rub it with liquid enzyme

detergent, then soak and agitate in cold water for
30 minutes or until the stain is removed.

6. Rinse well.

 7. Apply laundry presoak (spot stain remover) and let
stand several minutes.

 8. Launder according to garment label.

---

50.   **BEER**

General
Description:

*A beverage made by the brewing and fermentation of cereals,
usually malted barley, and flavored with hops and the like
for a slightly bitter taste.* Beer is one of the most popular
alcoholic beverages in the United States, Canada, Great
Britain, Ireland, and Germany. In Ireland a full 7 percent of the entire barley crop goes to the production of
Guinness, Ireland's most popular brew.

Season:

Beer is certainly a year-round drink, though different
types are popular at different times of the year. Lighter
beer, like pilsner and lager, is more popular in the
summer, when the heat makes for extreme thirst; darker,
heavier beer, like stout and porter, is more popular in
the winter. This means that beer stains will likely appear
throughout the year, though the color of the stains
will vary.

Areas of
Occurrence:

Spilled beer is an epidemic in bars across the land, which means that no part of your clothing is safe, from the seat of your jeans to the back of your jacket. Depending on the type of drinking game you play, you could even encounter beer stains in such out-of-the-way spots as underthings and socks.

Time of
Occurrence:

The hours between dusk and dawn are probably the most likely for you to experience a stain from beer, though it might not become apparent until the next day, when your vision may be clearer.

REMOVAL:

1. Rinse well.

2. Mix 1 teaspoon of a liquid enzyme detergent or dishwashing liquid with 1 cup of lukewarm water. (Do not use bar or natural soap of any kind on the fabric or the stain will set.) Pour mixture on stain and blot with an absorbent cloth. Replace the cloth as it becomes saturated.

3. Rinse well.

4. Make a mixture of 2 parts water to 1 part vinegar. Pour mixture on stain and blot quickly. Do not let the mixture sit on the fabric, since vinegar is a mild bleach.

5. Rinse well in warm water.

6. **Launder according to garment label.**

51. **COFFEE**

General
Description:

A drink made by percolation, infusion, or decoction from the roasted and ground or pounded seeds of several trees or shrubs (genus Coffea) of the madder family. Coffee has earned a special place among the favorite beverages worldwide, due in large part to its chemical makeup. Coffee contains a high percentage of caffeine, a substance that can help enforce alertness. Coffee is so important to humans that at about $115 (U.S.) a pound, Kopi Lewak coffee, grown in Indonesia, ranks as the most expensive beverage in the world.

Season:

Coffee stains transcend season, as coffee is available year-round and many people swear by it as the only remedy for morning or afternoon sleepiness.

Areas of
Occurrence:

Though it is a dangerous undertaking, many commuters hold cups or mugs of coffee between their legs as they ride or drive to work in the morning, making stains in this area especially likely. Other areas where stains are often found include furniture, jackets, coats, and the fronts of garments worn on the top of the body. Men may find that their neckties seem to seek out open cups of coffee, so that the tips are often at risk for stain.

Time of
Occurrence:

The coffee stain is not limited to any time of day or night. Hot coffee is an essential part of the morning ritual for many people. Some folks are so addicted to coffee that they'll continue to drink it all day and into the night. Many teenagers and college students drink coffee into the wee hours of the morning at "bottomless cup" diners and all-night restaurants—sometimes to stay awake to study, sometimes as a lubricant for conversation.

Variations of
Significance:

Café au lait; cappucino; chocolate-covered beans; coffee-flavored ice cream; latte

REMOVAL: *On fabric:*

1. Rinse back of stain well with cold water until you've removed as much stain as possible.

2. Rub a liquid enzyme detergent into the remaining stain and let stand several minutes. For old or dried stains, rub the stain with detergent, then soak the garment in cold water for up to 30 minutes or until the stain is loosened.

3. Launder with an enzyme detergent.

4. If the stain remains, rub it again with the enzyme detergent and soak garment in warm water for 10 to 15 minutes, then rinse well.

5. Apply a laundry presoak (spot stain remover) and let stand several minutes.

or

Make a paste of borax and water at a ratio of approximately 3 to 1 and spread it on the stain. Let stand 30 minutes, then brush off. Repeat until you have removed as much stain as possible.

6. Relaunder with enzyme detergent.

On carpet:

1. Blot as much liquid out of the carpet as possible.

2. Saturate stain with club soda or cold water, then blot again.

3. Apply a carpet spotter according to manufacturer's directions.

or

Spread non-gel shaving cream onto the stain and work into the carpet with an old toothbrush. Rinse with cold water or club soda, then blot.

or

Mix borax with warm water to make a paste at a ratio of approximately 3 to 1 and rub into stain. Let paste dry, then vacuum. Rinse with cold water or club soda, then blot.

4. If the stain remains, sponge with a mild bleach, such as white vinegar or hydrogen peroxide. Let stand 15 minutes.

5. Blot.

6. Sponge well with water or club soda and blot with a dry cloth.

52. SOFT DRINKS

General
Description:

Beverages that are not alcoholic or intoxicating and are usually carbonated, such as root beer, cola, or ginger ale. Coca-Cola is the most popular soft drink in the world, though perhaps it wouldn't be if food coloring weren't added during its processing: It would be green! When it was first introduced to China, Coca-Cola was marketed under the name "Ke-kou-ke-la." After thousands of advertisements had been printed, the company discovered that the name translated to "bite the wax tadpole" or "female horse stuffed with wax," depending on the dialect. The name was then changed to "Ko-kou-ko-le," which loosely translates to "happiness in the mouth."

Areas of
Occurrence:

Because sodas are carbonated and their bottles are tightly sealed, the probability that the pressure will build up and make them spray when opened is high; when this happens, all areas of clothing, furniture, walls, and flooring may fall victim to this stain.

Time of
Occurrence:

Die-hard soda drinkers may obtain this stain in the morning, but staining will usually occur in the afternoon or evening, when this beverage is most often consumed.

Variations of
Significance:

Mixed drinks; punch

REMOVAL:

For fresh stains on fabric:

1. Blot immediately with an absorbent cloth. Absorb as much liquid as possible.

2. Sponge or soak the stain with cold water.

3. Rub liquid enzyme detergent into stain. Let stand several minutes.

4. Launder in the hottest water safe for the fabric.

5. If the stain remains, apply a laundry presoak (spot stain remover), then launder, adding a bleach that is safe for the fabric. Test first for colorfastness.

For dried stains on fabric:

1. Soften the stain by rubbing glycerin into the cloth.

2. Let stand for 30 minutes. If glycerin is not available, soak the stain in a sudsy liquid enzyme detergent mixture until the stain is loosened.

3. Rinse well in cold water.

4. Follow steps 3 through 5 for fresh stains, above.

On carpet:

1. Blot immediately with an absorbent cloth. Absorb as much liquid as possible.

2. Sponge with a sudsy mixture of liquid laundry detergent and cold water. Continue until you have removed as much stain as possible.

3. Sponge with a clean, damp cloth, then let dry.

4. Vacuum.

5. If the stain remains, repeat steps 2 through 4 as needed.

6. If the stain remains, apply a carpet spotter according to manufacturer's directions.

53. **TEA**

General
Description:
An aromatic beverage prepared from the leaves, leaf buds, and internodes of a shrub (Camellia sinensis *of the family* Theaceae) *by infusion with boiling water.* Tea can also be made from a number of other herbs—it is then called "herbal tea." Teas have played a central role in many cultures around the world. In Chinese and Japanese cultures, elaborate ceremonies created thousands of years ago focused on the consumption of tea. In 1773 American colonists revolted against the British in response to excessive taxes levied on tea. In contemporary times, an American consumes only around 150 cups per year. Britain ranks second in the world behind Ireland for tea drinking. While the Irish consume an average of 1,390 cups per person each year, the average Brit consumes 1,113 cups per year.

Season:

Tea is consumed year-round, and stains therefore may be attained at any time. Hot tea is popular during the colder months, while iced tea is a standard beverage during summer. There is an increase in tea drinking (and in turn, staining) during flu-and-cold season, when doctors recommend drinking tea with lemon to aid in respiration and to ward off fever.

Areas of
Occurrence:
Tea stains are often found on furniture, jackets, and coats, the lap areas of pants, and on the fronts of garments worn on the top of the body. Men may find that

the fronts and cuffs of clean, starched white shirts are particularly at risk, as well as the tips of neckties, which seem to seek out open cups.

Time of
Occurrence:

Tea stains can be found morning, noon, and night. Some herbal varieties are popular at night before bedtime, and at this sleepy hour you must be particularly vigilant against staining.

REMOVAL: *On fabric:*

 1. Rinse back of stain well with cold water until you've removed as much as possible.

2. Rub a liquid enzyme detergent into the remaining stain and let stand several minutes. For old or dried stains, rub the stain with detergent, then soak the garment in cold water for up to 30 minutes or until the stain is loosened.

 3. Launder with an enzyme detergent.

4. If the stain remains, rub the stain again with the enzyme detergent, soak garment in warm water for 10 to 15 minutes.

 5. Rinse well.

 6. Apply a laundry presoak (spot stain remover) and

let stand several minutes.

or

Make a paste of borax and water at a ratio of approximately 3 to 1 and spread it onto the stain. Let stand 30 minutes, then brush off. Repeat until you have removed as much stain as possible.

 7. Relaunder with enzyme detergent.

On carpet:

1. Blot as much liquid out of the carpet as possible.

2. Saturate stain with club soda or cold water, then blot again.

3. Apply a carpet spotter according to manufacturer's directions.

or

Spread non-gel shaving cream onto the stain and work into the carpet with an old toothbrush. Rinse with cold water or club soda, then blot.

or

 Mix borax with warm water to make a paste at a ratio of approximately 3 to 1 and rub into stain. Let paste dry, then vacuum. Rinse with cold water or club soda, then blot.

 4. If the stain remains, sponge with a mild bleach,

such as white vinegar or hydrogen peroxide. Let
stand 15 minutes.

5. Blot with a dry cloth.

6. Sponge well with water or club soda, then blot.

---

54. **TOMATO JUICE**

General
Description:

*The thick liquid that comes from squeezing the mildly
acidic pulpy berry known as a tomato, drunk as juice.*
Popular as both a healthy breakfast drink and a mixer
used with alcohol, tomato juice is also the official state
beverage of Ohio. Though its primary use is as a drink,
tomato juice is also useful for getting smells off pets—if
a dog is sprayed by a skunk, the sure cure is a bath in
tomato juice!

Season:

Tomato juice is popular at breakfast tables and in
Bloody Marys year round, and its stains won't be confined to a particular season.

Areas of
Occurrence:

The lap areas of pants, skirts, and shorts are prime
targets for this stain, which is thick, though also runny.
Other areas that might fall victim to this stain are cuffs
of blouses and jackets, as well as nightgowns and pajamas.

REMOVAL: 1. Use a dull knife or spoon to remove as much as possible.

2. Flush the back of the stain immediately with cold water to force stain through fabric.

3. Rub a liquid enzyme detergent into the stain and let stand several minutes. Rub the fabric between thumbs, then rinse well.

4. Sponge with a mild bleach, such as white vinegar, hydrogen peroxide, or lemon juice, then rinse well.

5. Repeat steps 3 and 4 until no more stain can be removed.

6. Apply a laundry presoak (spot stain remover) and let stand several minutes.

7. Launder with an enzyme detergent.

8. Let garment dry in the sun for added bleaching.

9. If the stain remains, rub an enzyme detergent into the stain and then soak garment in warm water for up to 30 minutes or until the stain is gone.

10. Rinse well.

II. **Apply laundry presoak (spot stain remover) and relaunder.**

55. **WINE, RED**

General
Description:

A fermented juice made from black grapes, which derives its color from the contact between the juice and the grape skins during fermentation; the colors range from pink to dark red. Merlot and Cabernet Sauvignon are popular varieties. The strong, bold flavors of red wine produce just as strong and unwieldy stains. It seems strange that heavy stains can come from a liquid that will spoil if exposed to light—indeed, many wine bottles are tinted because direct sunlight can ruin even the heartiest of wines.

Season:

Though red wine is served year-round, most people prefer to drink the heartier red wines in fall and winter. Stains are often found on the formal attire of those attending holiday parties, and on the carpets and rugs of those hosting these holiday gatherings. Red wines are also a year-round favorite as an accompaniment to Italian meals and entrees featuring red meat.

Areas of
Occurrence:

Staining may be anywhere on the fronts of shirts and dresses, as well as splashed on pant legs and skirts as the hours grow later. You must allow for the eventuality that someone at your party will place her glass on the floor next to her chair and promptly kick it over, spilling the glass's contents onto the floor. Another common spot for occurrence are the altar garments and clothes worn by Communion participants at Catholic masses.

Time of Occurrence:

With the possible exception of early morning, depending upon drinking preference, red-wine stains often seem to appear as if from nowhere. During a particularly engaging dinner party or gathering of friends, they may not be detected until later in the evening, or even the next morning, depending upon the amount consumed. As previously noted, you must be particularly vigilant during the winter holiday season.

Variations of Significance:

Coq au vin; beef bourguignon; pasta sauces; red-wine vinaigrettes; sangria

REMOVAL: *On fabric:*

1. Pour white wine, club soda, or cold water on the stain immediately.

2. Blot with an absorbent cloth, then sprinkle salt onto the stain and let stand 1 to 2 minutes.

3. Rinse in cold water and rub out the stain.

4. If the stain remains, repeat steps 1 through 3 until no more stain can be removed.

5. Rub a liquid enzyme detergent into the stain and let stand several minutes.

 6. Rinse with cold water.

 7. If the stain remains, apply a laundry presoak (spot stain remover).

 8. Launder with a liquid enzyme detergent.

On carpet:

1. Blot up as much wine as possible with an absorbent cloth.

2. Saturate the stain with club soda or cold water.

3. Repeat steps 1 and 2 as needed.

4. If the stain remains, make a paste of borax or baking soda and water at a ratio of approximately 3 to 1. Smear paste onto stain with an old toothbrush and let dry.

 5. Vacuum.

6. Repeat until no more stain can be removed.

7. If the stain remains, treat with a carpet spotter.

56.   **WINE, WHITE**

General
Description:

A fermented juice made from white (and occasionally, red) grapes; there is minimal, if any, contact between the juice and the skins during fermentation; its color can vary from pale to almost amber. Chardonnay, Pinot Grigio, and Sauvignon Blanc are popular varieties. White wine is often best served chilled, but only for about two hours—refrigerating white wine or champagne for more than a few hours can dull both the flavor and the bouquet.

Season:

White wine is best drunk with light fare, such as poultry and fish, and dishes that are most popular during the summer months. Champagne is the customary drink at any big celebration, especially New Year's Eve, but since the good times aren't limited by season, neither is the potential for a white-wine stain.

Areas of
Occurrence:

This stain is found anywhere on the fronts of shirts and dresses, as well as splashed on pant legs and skirts. You must allow for the eventuality of another person accidentally knocking his glass into your back, causing stains that are difficult to detect unless you are completely drenched in the stuff.

Time of
Occurrence:

The white-wine stain is a member of that class wherein the times of acquisition and the times of discovery are very different. They are most likely to be achieved during

the evening and late-night hours, when parties, celebrations, and bars are often visited. Society dictates that
you would never obtain a stain from white wine before
10 A.M., with the exception of an occasional Mimosa.

Variations of
Significance:

Champagne; champagne cocktails; marinades and
sauces; some sangrias; white-wine vinegar

REMOVAL:

1. Rinse back of stain well with cold water or club soda.

2. If the stain remains, rub with dishwashing liquid
   or liquid enzyme detergent. Let stand several minutes. (Do not use bar or natural soap of any kind
   or the stain will set.)

3. Rinse well with cold water.

4. Launder according to garment label.

5. If the stain remains, rub it with liquid enzyme
   detergent, then soak and agitate in cold water for
   30 minutes or until the stain is removed.

6. Rinse well.

7. Apply laundry presoak (spot stain remover) and let
   stand several minutes.

8. Launder according to garment label.

Household Items and Miscellany

57. **AMMONIA**

General
Description:
A colorless, pungent, highly water-soluble, gaseous compound, used chiefly for refrigeration and in the manufacture of commercial chemicals and laboratory reagents.
Ammonia gets its name from the Salt of Ammon, a hard, white, crystalline salt supposed to have been originally prepared from the dung of camels near the temple of Jupiter Ammon, not far from the Jordan River. Many cleansers sold in supermarkets and drugstores contain ammonia or ammonia compounds, making it a widely used staining agent.

Season:

Spring is perhaps the most common time for this stain, as spring cleaning is a practice that still engages scores of neat-freaks across the land during the first months of the season. However, since cleaning is not limited to these months, ammonia stains will crop up throughout the year.

Areas of
Occurrence:

This stain's placement depends on how vigorously you clean. For dedicated scrubbers of floors, the knees of sweatpants or jeans will bear the brunt of this stain. Since cleansers are often liquid or diluted with water and can splash, however, ammonia stains may appear anywhere on T-shirts or sweatshirts as well.

REMOVAL: 1. Rinse the back of the stain thoroughly with cold water.

2. Mix equal amounts of white vinegar and water and sponge the stain with the mixture.

 3. Rinse in warm water.

4. Repeat steps 2 through 3 as needed.

 5. Launder according to garment label.

---

58. **BLEACH**

General
Description:
A chemical agent used to make a surface or fabric white or colorless. Bleach stains are one of the most paradoxical, because they're usually acquired when cleaning or when working to remove another stain. A popular brand of bleach in the United States is Clorox, which got its name from combining the words "chlorine" and "sodium hydroxide," two substances that, when mixed, form bleach's active ingredient, sodium hypochlorite.

Season:
Since there is always laundry to do, and since there are many stubborn stains that are best treated with bleach, bleach stains may present themselves at any time of year.

Areas of Occurrence:

Bleach is a dangerous substance that can stain in any number of ways, in any number of areas. If using the bleach as a spot cleaner, you may find that it has removed more than just the color of the offending stain. If you are bleaching an entire load of laundry, chances for accidentally staining socks, colored T-shirts, or a stray pair of pants increase. Because bleach is often sold in large jugs, it tends to splatter when being poured, often staining shirts or pants.

Variations of Significance:

Hair bleach; kitchen and bathroom, counter and tile cleaners

REMOVAL: *On fabric:*

1. Rinse the back of the stain immediately and thoroughly with cold water to neutralize the acid.

2. Place garment on an absorbent cloth and sponge well with ammonia, starting from the outside of the stain's edge. Replace cloth underneath as it becomes saturated. (If treating stains on wool or silk, dilute ammonia with an equal amount of cold water.) If ammonia is not available, substitute a baking soda paste, mixing baking soda and water at a ratio of approximately 3 to 1. Rub onto stain.

3. Rinse well.

4. Repeat as needed.

5. Launder according to garment label.

On carpet:

1. Sponge the stain immediately with cold water to remove as much acid as possible.

2. Mix baking soda and water to make a paste at a ratio of approximately 3 to 1 and scrub into stain with an old toothbrush, then let dry.

3. Repeat steps 1 and 2 until you have removed as much stain as possible.

4. Vacuum.

59. **DYES OR RUNNING COLORS**

General Description:

A coloring material, used on clothing to produce a specific hue or tint. Because dye is designed to be absorbed into cloth, it becomes a problem in the washing machine and dryer. When colors run or dyes are transferred from one item of clothing to another, they can form a stain. Recently some laundry detergent brands have introduced new products that claim to reduce running colors, or to even absorb extra dye that may "leak" from clothing.

Season: Washing clothes, as well as dyeing or tie-dyeing them, is
              a year-round activity; thus this stain isn't limited to a
              specific time of year.

Areas of   When dyeing clothing in your home, you may experience
Occurrence: a splash or splatter that affects the wrong clothing—

              namely the clothes you are wearing rather than the item
              you are dyeing. Therefore a dye stain can appear just
              about anywhere on jeans, T-shirts, or shorts. When a
              stain of this nature occurs in the laundry process, it may
              be everywhere and anywhere, from the backs of blouses
              to the armpits of a favorite sweater.

REMOVAL: 1. Dilute bleach according to label and soak the

              stained garment in a non-metal container for 6 to 8
              hours or until the stain is removed. Check first for
              colorfastness. If color is affected, spread garment
              over a container in the sink and let cold water slowly
              drip onto the stain. Drain the container as needed.
              Continue for 3 to 4 hours.

           2. If the stain remains, sponge with equal parts
              hydrogen peroxide and water and lay garment in
              the sun. Keep moist with peroxide solution until
              the stain is gone. Test first for colorfastness.

           3. Rinse well, then launder according to garment label.

           4. If the stain remains, repeat steps 1 through 3.

60. **FOOD COLORING**

General
Description:

One of about three dozen or so naturally occurring or synthetic food additives used to alter and intensify color in a processed food. Food coloring is most often associated with the baking and crafts that accompany any of a number of holidays. Sometimes entire cities can be in on the activity—the city of Chicago started coloring the Chicago River green on St. Patrick's Day in 1962, when 100 pounds of green vegetable dye were added, keeping the water green for a week. Today, 40 pounds of green food coloring keep the river green for a few hours.

Season:

Food coloring can be used in crafts year-round, but it is most commonly seen around holidays. Many people color Easter eggs in March and April, staining hands, shirts, carpets, and anything else that might get in the way. Food coloring is also common during the Christmas and Hanukkah baking seasons. A particularly risky day for food-coloring stains is March 17, St. Patrick's Day, when many people add green food coloring to beer to show their true Irish colors (and end up with trails of wayward color on the fronts of their shirts).

Areas of
Occurrence:

In addition to the potential targets noted above, you should be careful of your apron, table cloth, carpet, and all areas of exposed clothing while coloring Easter eggs, especially when in the company of small children.

Time of Occurrence:	Most peoples' baking or craft making that involves food coloring takes place during the day. However, when green beer is involved, the revelry can last from early morning to the wee hours of the following day, when the luck of the Irish just might run out.
Variations of Significance:	Candy; cookies; frosting

REMOVAL: *On fabric:*

1. Treat the stain as soon as possible. Hold stain upside down under a stream of cold water to force food coloring out of fabric. Continue until no more coloring is removed.

2. If the stain remains, rub a liquid enzyme detergent into it and let stand several minutes. Agitate the fabric, rubbing the stain between your thumbs.

3. Rinse well in cold water.

4. Repeat steps 2 and 3 until you've removed as much food coloring as possible.

5. Apply laundry presoak (spot stain remover) and let stand several minutes.

6. Launder according to garment label.

7. If the stain remains, mix equal parts of hydrogen peroxide and water and sponge mixture onto stain. Place stain in sunlight and keep moist with peroxide solution until the stain is removed.

8. Rinse well.

On carpet:

1. Blot stain well with an absorbent cloth.

2. Sponge the stain with club soda or cold water. Repeat until you have removed as much stain as possible.

3. Treat with a carpet spotter, according to manufacturer's directions.

4. If the stain remains, blot with a mild bleach such as hydrogen peroxide or lemon juice, then sponge with cold water. Repeat as needed.

61. **FURNITURE POLISH**

General
Description:

A substance that protects and beautifies fine woodwork and antiques, giving smoothness or gloss to them. Most commercial polishes contains petroleum distillates, which are harmful when inhaled. You can, however, make your own natural furniture polish by combining two parts vegetable or olive oil with one part lemon juice. (See OIL, COOKING OR VEGETABLE on page 86 and LEMON JUICE on page 24.) Any polish you use should be rubbed onto finished furniture in the direction of the grain, using a soft, lint-free cloth.

Areas of
Occurrence:

Furniture polish is generally sold in spray cans or bottles. The area of the stain may determine which type you choose. Spray cans will likely not cause as many stains as the bottled types of polish, but misdirected spray can mar the fronts of T-shirts and pants. Bottled polish is more difficult to control, and will therefore stain more frequently. Sleeves and elbows of sweatshirts and T-shirts are most vulnerable to this stain, especially when polishing is vigorous.

Time of
Occurrence:

Any time furniture becomes dull, dingy, or scratched is a time when this stain can occur.

REMOVAL: *On fabric:*

1. **Blot excess with absorbent cloth.**

2. **Spray stain with WD-40™ and let stand for 10 minutes.**

3. **Sponge with dishwashing liquid and tepid water, occasionally rubbing the stain between your thumbs.**

4. Rinse well.

5. Repeat steps 2 through 4 until you have removed as much stain as possible.

6. If the stain remains, apply a laundry presoak (spot stain remover) and let stand several minutes.

7. Launder in the hottest water safe for the fabric.

8. If a color stain remains, dilute bleach according to label and soak the stained garment in a non-metal container for 6 to 8 hours or until the stain is removed. Check first for colorfastness. If color is affected, spread garment over a container in the sink and let cold water slowly drip onto the stain. Drain the container as needed. Continue for 3 to 4 hours.

9. If the stain remains, sponge with equal parts hydrogen peroxide and water and lay garment in the sun. Keep moist with peroxide solution until the stain is gone. Test first for colorfastness.

10. Rinse well and launder according to garment label.

On carpet:

1. Blot excess with an absorbent cloth.

2. Sponge with dishwashing liquid and tepid water.

3. Scrub soapy mixture lightly into stain with an old toothbrush.

4. Blot with a damp cloth.

5. Repeat steps 2 through 4 until you have removed as much as possible.

6. Sponge with clean water, then blot with a dry cloth.

7. If the stain remains, treat with a carpet spotter according to manufacturer's directions.

62. **GUM**

General Description:

A sweetened, flavored substance for chewing, usually made of chicle. The popularity of chewing gum spread during World War II, when U.S. military personnel shared and traded gum with people in Europe, Asia, and Africa. Its traditional pink color is credited to chance—the inventor had only pink coloring left, and the color has "stuck" through the years. Gum's sticky nature doesn't affect only fabric—many people encounter the disastrous problem of removing chewing gum from hair. The most reliable method—aside from using scissors—involves peanut butter. Massage a small amount of peanut butter—preferably smooth, though chunky will work—into the gum until it is loose enough to remove. Then you must battle the peanut butter in your hair. (See PEANUT BUTTER on page 45.)

Season:

Chewing gum will adhere to clothes, carpets, and furniture regardless of season, but there is an increased chance of encountering the substance during the school year, when children are likely to try to hide gum from strict teachers and principals. Another time when the incidence of this stain may be higher is in January, when New Year's resolutions are in place and smokers are desperate to kick the habit, and in November, during the Great American Smoke-Out.

Areas of Occurrence:

Gum is most often found on shoes, the seats of pants, and chairs and other upholstered furniture, though strings of gum might stick anywhere. No parts of pants, fronts of shirts, dresses, and school uniforms are safe. Gum can also be found on bedsheets and pillowcases if you fall asleep with gum in your mouth.

Time of Occurrence:

School hours, from about 8 A.M. to 3 P.M., are the most common time for gum to stick to clothing and other materials, but any time someone is fighting the urge for a smoke can also create a sticky situation.

Variations of Significance:

Bubble gum ice cream

REMOVAL: *On fabric:*

1. Place an ice cube in a plastic bag and rub over the gum until it hardens. (Or place entire garment in the freezer.)

2. Use a dull knife or spoon to remove as much as possible.

3. If the stain remains, treat it with a laundry presoak (spot stain remover) and let stand several minutes.

4. Rub a liquid laundry detergent into the stain and launder according to garment label.

5. If the stain remains, repeat step 3, then launder with a bleach that is safe for the fabric.

On carpet:

1. Place an ice cube in a plastic bag and rub over the gum until it hardens. Use a dull knife or spoon to remove as much as possible.

2. If the stain remains, treat with a carpet spotter. Use according to manufacturer's directions.

Color Plates

Color Guide to Stains

Stains and colors go hand in hand, and determining your culprit is sometimes simply a matter of color identification. Refer to this chart to find the top five items in each stain color.

RED

Blood
Fruits or Berries
Ketchup
Salsa
Vinegar

GREEN

Broccoli
Grass
Relish
Spinach
Vomit

ORANGE

Barbecue or Steak Sauces
Carrot
Potato, Sweet
Rust
Sap

BLUE

Fruits or Berries
Ink, all types
Paint, all types
Toothpaste
Windshield Wiper Fluid

YELLOW

Adhesives or Stickers
Beer
Mustard
Pollen
Sweat

PURPLE

Cabbage, Red
Fruits or Berries
Jam or Jelly
Onion, Red
Wine, Red

PINK

- Gum
- Lipstick
- Medicine
- Wax, Candle
- Yogurt

BROWN

- Chocolate
- Coffee
- Dirt or Mud
- Iodine
- Soy Sauce

BLACK

- Charcoal
- Grease
- Ink, all types
- Soot or Smoke
- Tar or Asphalt

CLEAR/TRANSLUCENT

- Dairy Products
- Gasoline
- Oil, all types
- Ointment
- Wine, White

WHITE

- Correction Fluid
- Deodorants or Antiperspirants
- Glue
- Lotion, Hand or Body
- Semen

Stains Icon Key

Season	Areas of Occurance	Removal	
--------	--------------------	---------	
☀ spring	shirt	water	▲ bleach
☼ summer	tie	SOAP bar of soap	lemon
🍁 fall	jacket	launder	spray bottle
❄ winter	skirt	iron	absorbent
	pants	vacuum	tea kettle

Temperature indicators: • cold   • • warm   • • • hot

1. avocado

2. baby food

3. baked beans

4. beet

5. broccoli

6. red cabbage

7. carrot

8. fruits or berries

9. jam or jelly

10. lemon juice

11. red onion

12. red pepper

13. sweet potato

14. spinach

15. squash

16. tomato

17. zucchini

18. egg

19. animal fats

20. hummus

21. peanut butter

22. tuna fish

23. baby formula

24. butter or margarine

25. cheese

26. ice cream

27. milk or cream

28. pudding

29. sour cream

30. yogurt

31. steak sauce

32. caramel

33. chocolate

34. gravy

35. honey

36. ketchup

37. maple syrup

38. mayonnaise

39. mustard

40. vegetable oil

41. relish

42. creamy dressing

43. vinaigrette

44. salsa

45. soy sauce

46. tomato sauce

47. vinegar

48. worcestershire sauce

49. alcoholic beverage

50. beer

51. coffee

52. soft drink

53. tea

54. tomato juice

55. red wine

56. white wine

57. ammonia

58. bleach

59. color dye

60. food coloring

61. furniture polish

62. gum

63. hydrogen peroxide

64. iodine

65. medicine

66. mildew

67. acrylic paint

68. oil paint

69. rust

70. scorch marks

71. shoe polish

72. soot

73. tarnish

74. tobacco

75. water spots

76. candle wax

77. yellowing

78. charcoal

79. dirt or mud

80. gasoline

81. grass

82. grease

83. motor oil

84. pollen

85. sap

86. tar

87. wiper fluid

88. blood

89. excrement

90. ring around the collar

91. semen

92. sweat

93. urine

94. vomit

95. baby oil

96. blush or rouge

97. deodorant

98. eyeliner

99. foundation

100. lip balm

101. lipstick

102. body lotion

103. mascara

104. nail polish

105. ointment

106. perfume

107. toothpaste

108. adhesive

109. copier toner

110. chalk

111. correction fluid

112. crayon

113. model airplane glue

114. rubber cement

115. water-based glue

116. ballpoint ink

117. permanent ink

118. water-based ink

119. pencil

63.   **HYDROGEN PEROXIDE**

General
Description:
An aqueous solution used chiefly as an antiseptic and a bleaching agent that is derived from a colorless, unstable, oily liquid. There's nothing better for use on a cut or scrape than hydrogen peroxide, even though it stings when applied. Hydrogen peroxide is a natural healer—it must be present in the body for the immune system to function properly. White blood cells produce it as the first line of defense against toxins, parasites, bacteria, viruses, and yeast.

Season:
Since there is no prescribed time of year for mishaps resulting in skin abrasions, there is no set season when a hydrogen peroxide stain will be more likely. The exception might be summer, when the number of cuts and scrapes may rise with the temperature, since shorts are worn and children play outside more at that time.

Areas of
Occurrence:

When treating a scrape on the knee with the stuff, the rolled up cuffs of pant legs or the hems of shorts will be most affected by this stain. When hair dye is unavailable, hydrogen peroxide works to bleach hair. In this instance, the stain will be found on the collar area of whatever type of shirt is worn during the dyeing process.

REMOVAL: *On fabric:*

1. Rinse the back of the stain thoroughly as soon as possible with cold water to neutralize the acid.

2. Place garment on an absorbent cloth and sponge well with ammonia, starting from the outside of the stain's edge. Replace cloth underneath as it becomes saturated. (If treating stains on wool or silk, dilute ammonia with an equal amount of cold water.) If ammonia is not available, substitute a baking soda paste, mixing baking soda and water at a ratio of approximately 3 to 1. Rub into stain.

3. Rinse well.

4. Repeat as needed.

 5. Launder according to garment label.

On carpet:

1. Sponge the stain immediately with cold water to remove as much acid as possible.

2. Mix baking soda and water to make a paste at a ratio of approximately 3 to 1 and scrub into stain with an old toothbrush, then let dry.

3. Repeat steps 1 and 2 until you have removed as much stain as possible.

 4. Vacuum.

64. **IODINE**

General
Description:

A liquid containing iodine, a grayish-black, corrosive, poisonous element, dissolved in ethyl alcohol, used as an antiseptic for wounds. Iodine gets its name from the Greek word *Iôdes*, meaning "violet," since it gives off a violet vapor when heated. Iodine itself is a poisonous gas, as are the related halogens chlorine, fluorine, and bromine. However, as with chlorine, the salts are negatively charged ions of iodine (iodides). It is this not-so-disruptive form of iodine that is used to clean cuts and wounds.

Season:

Summertime is iodine season. You are most likely to encounter scrapes, cuts, and scratches during this active time of year, when working or playing outdoors. Of course, the less graceful among us can encounter such scrapes and cuts regardless of the season, and there are few who can escape a paper cut during the dry winter months. Iodine transcends season in these instances—it is a stain-maker for all seasons.

Areas of
Occurrence:

Iodine stains aren't just found on the lab coats of chemists. Stains can sneak out from underneath bandages on any part of the body, but most likely on knees, elbows, and other scrape-prone areas, to stain shorts and T-shirts. Bedsheets are at particular risk for iodine stains because, in the quest to let a wound breathe, you may not bandage a wound that has been covered in iodine, leading to the morning surprise of stained bed linens.

REMOVAL: 1. Rinse back of stain well with cold water.

2. Place stain-down on an absorbent cloth and blot with sudsy mixture of liquid laundry detergent and water. Replace the cloth beneath as it becomes saturated. Continue until no more iodine is removed.

  3. Rinse well.

 4. If the stain remains, blot with a mild bleach, such as vinegar, hydrogen peroxide, or lemon juice.

5. Rinse well.

6. Blot again with detergent mixture from step 2.

 7. Rinse well.

8. Launder according to garment label.

9. If the stain remains, set in sunlight to dry, then repeat steps 2 through 7.

65. **MEDICINE**

General
Description:

Any substance used in treating disease or illness. While medication can be found in many forms, such as pills, powder, syrup, and suppository, the only kind that will stain clothing and other fabrics is the syrup. Cough and cold syrups are sold over the counter in most drugstores and come in a variety of strengths and flavors.

Season:

Though a cold or cough can be caught any time of year, fall and winter are most often associated with the cold season.

Areas of
Occurrence:

Since syrups are viscous and those taking them are likely to be at least partially incapacitated due to illness, stains from them can be far-reaching. Dribbled cough syrup is likely to be found on the fronts of T-shirts, pajama tops, and nightgowns, as well as on robes, socks, sheets, and bed linens, depending on the awareness—or lack thereof—of the person administering the fluid.

REMOVAL: *For iron tonics:*

1. Apply a mild bleach, such as lemon juice, to the stain.

2. Sprinkle with salt to absorb stain. For colored fabrics, test first for colorfastness before completing steps 1 and 2.

3. Let fabric sit in direct sunlight. The sun will help to bleach out the stain. Test first for colorfastness.

4. Repeat steps 1 through 3 until stain is removed. Do not let the stain dry between applications.

5. Rinse well in warm water.

6. Launder according to garment label.

7. If the stain remains, treat with a rust remover according to manufacturer's directions.

For alcohol-based medicines:

1. Rinse back of stain well with cold water or club soda.

2. If the stain remains, rub with liquid dishwashing soap or liquid enzyme detergent. Let stand several minutes. (Do not use bar or natural soap of any kind or the stain will set.)

3. Rinse well with cold water.

4. Launder according to garment label.

5. If the stain remains, rub it with liquid enzyme detergent, then soak and agitate in cold water for 30 minutes or until the stain is removed.

6. Rinse well.

 7. Apply laundry presoak (spot stain remover) and let stand several minutes.

 8. Launder according to garment label.

For oil-based medicines:

1. Use a dull knife or spoon to remove as much as possible.

2. Blot remaining liquid with an absorbent cloth.

 3. Sprinkle salt, baking soda, cornstarch, or talcum powder on stain to absorb excess, let stand 10 to 15 minutes, then brush off.

4. Rub colorless dishwashing liquid into stain. Let stand 1 to 2 minutes.

5. Soak in a sudsy mixture of hot water and dishwashing liquid for up to 30 minutes.

 6. Rinse the back of the stain well with hot water.

7. Use a dull knife or spoon again to remove any loosened material from the fabric.

8. If the stain remains, repeat steps 3 through 7 until no more can be removed. Alternatively, make a paste of baking soda and water at a ratio of approximately 3 to 1, spread on stain and let dry, then brush off.

9. Apply laundry presoak (spot stain remover) and let stand several minutes to penetrate fabric.

10. Launder in the hottest water safe for the fabric. For extra-heavy stains, replace half the amount of detergent with baking soda.

---

66. **MILDEW**

General
Description: *Any of various fungi that form a grayish substance and usually grow on materials like cloth and paper.* Mildew is often used interchangeably with the word "mold." Both are generic terms that describe a variety of microorganisms, including fungi, algae, rusts, yeasts, and bacteria. Mildew requires three elements to survive and thrive: a warm climate, a food source, and moisture, making it a natural enemy to campers, homemakers, and college students everywhere.

Season: Mildew is prevalent in the warmer periods of the spring, summer, and fall, when both visits to the swimming pool and rain are more likely. These factors alone don't bring the mildew—they work in combo with neglecting to take wet clothes out of your gym bag. Spring, summer, and fall are also seasons for camping, which, with its accompanying lack of clothes dryers and hangers, can provide a fertile breeding ground for mildew.

Areas of Occurrence:
Mildew does not discriminate. It can manifest anywhere on clothes, towels, jackets, upholstered car seats, in the car trunk, on basement carpeting (or any carpeting that is located in a warm, damp place), on bathroom tiles, and shower curtains.

REMOVAL: *On fabric:*

1. Take garment outside and shake well. Mildew, like other fungi, reproduces via millions of tiny spores. Do not shake a mildewed garment indoors.

2. Soak the stain in cold water until the stain is loosened.

3. Rub liquid laundry detergent into the stain.

4. Launder in the hottest water that is safe for the fabric, with a bleach that is also safe for the fabric.

5. Dry thoroughly, preferably in the sun.

6. If the stain remains, sponge the fabric with lemon juice, sprinkle with salt, then set in the sun to dry.

7. If the stain remains, rinse well and repeat steps 3 through 6.

On tile:

1. Make sure that the room is well ventilated before treating the mildew. Spray a tile cleaner on the tiles and shower curtain according to manufacturer's directions, or pour white vinegar into a spray bottle and spray the tiles and shower curtain.

2. Scrub with a brush or sponge.

3. Rinse well with water.

4. If the stain remains, mix a 10 percent bleach solution and pour it into a spray bottle. Spray the bleach mixture onto the stain. Let stand several minutes, then rinse well with water.

---

67. **PAINT, ACRYLIC OR WATER-BASED**

General Description:

A substance composed of solid coloring matter suspended in a liquid medium and applied as a protective or decorative coating to various surfaces, or to canvas or other materials in producing a work of art. Acrylic paints and other water-based paints dissolve in water (rather than oil, as in oil-based paints), which makes them a favorite for parents and teachers when painting with children. Nearly everyone remembers art classes from grade school, with or without fondness. Whether they've enjoyed creating colorful canvases or dreaded it, most people can remember a time when a pesky paint stain was no one's idea of a work of art.

Season:

Painting the house is generally a spring and summer activity, so stains incurred during this activity will generally happen in those seasons. Artwork, however, knows no season, and stains that arise during this endeavor can happen at any time of year.

Areas of
Occurrence:

You should wear protective or old clothing no matter the type of painting, but there is still a chance that a stain will appear unexpectedly. Since large surfaces are often painted, stains may appear on the backs as well as on the fronts of T-shirts, sweatshirts, and jeans.

REMOVAL: *For fresh stains on fabric:*

1. Use a dull knife or spoon to remove as much as possible.

2. Blot stain with an absorbent cloth. Keep the stain moist for best results.

3. Sponge the stain with a sudsy detergent mixture and rinse. Rub the stain between your thumbs.

4. Rinse well.

5. Repeat steps 3 and 4 until you have removed as much stain as possible.

6. If the stain remains, blot with nail polish remover on an absorbent cloth.

7. Rinse well.

For dried stains on fabric:

1. Brush off as much paint as possible.

2. Apply soapy water or an acrylic paint and varnish remover.

3. Once the stain has softened, use a dull knife or spoon to remove as much as possible. Test first for colorfastness.

4. Rinse well.

5. See steps 2 through 7 for fresh stains.

On carpet:

1. Use a dull knife or spoon to remove as much as possible.

2. Blot stain with an absorbent cloth. Keep the stain moist for best results. If paint has already dried, brush off as much as possible, then apply soapy water or an acrylic paint and varnish remover. Once the stain has softened, use a dull knife or spoon to remove as much as possible. Test first for colorfastness. For large spills, saturate the stain with water and lay towels and other absorbent cloths over the area to blot. Walk on the towels to help absorb as much paint as possible.

3. Rinse well.

4. Blot the stain with rubbing alcohol.

5. Rinse well.

6. Repeat steps 2 through 5 until you have removed as much stain as possible.

7. If the stain remains, dampen sponge and apply a laundry presoak (spot stain remover). Let stand several minutes.

8. Rinse well.

68.   **PAINT, OIL-BASED**

General
Description:

A liquid mixture that use pigments originally ground in oil and breaks down when subjected to oil. Many a cleanup in the studio has led to slippery, oily messes (see OIL, COOKING OR VEGETABLE on page 86) because oil paint is difficult to clean. It also lasts longer; the paintings passed down from the great masters were painted with oil-based paints. X rays of the Mona Lisa show that there are three completely different versions of the same subject, all painted by Leonardo, under the final portrait.

Areas of
Occurrence:

Literally any spot on a painter's body is vulnerable to this stain, from the top of a beret to the bottom of a shoe, and anywhere in between.

Time of
Occurrence:

Artists are forced to act when the muse strikes, therefore the time of a stain's occurrence is not predictable.

REMOVAL:

For fresh stains on fabric:

1. Use a dull knife or spoon to remove as much as possible.

2. Blot stain with an absorbent cloth. Keep the stain moist for best results.

   3. Rinse well.

4. Place fabric stain-side down on an absorbent cloth and sponge the back of the stain with turpentine. Test first for colorfastness. Replace the cloth underneath as it becomes saturated. Continue until no more paint is removed. Do not rinse the stain.

5. Rub liquid laundry detergent into any remaining stain and soak garment in hot water overnight. Occasionally rub the stain between your thumbs during soaking.

6. Rinse well.

7. Launder according to garment label.

8. If the stain remains, apply a laundry presoak (spot stain remover) and let stand several minutes.

9. Launder according to garment label.

For dried stains on fabric:

1. Brush off as much as possible.

2. Read the paint can label to obtain a recomended paint-and-varnish remover for thinning the paint, then apply.

3. Once the stain has softened, use a dull knife or

spoon to remove as much as possible.

4. Follow steps 2 through 9 for fresh stains, above.

On carpet:

 1. Use a dull knife or spoon to remove as much as possible, then blot stain with an absorbent cloth. Keep the stain moist for best results. If paint has already dried, brush off as much as possible. Read the paint can label to obtain a recommended paint-and-varnish remover for thinning the paint, then apply. Once the stain has softened, use a dull knife or spoon to remove as much as possible. Test first for colorfastness. Rinse well.

2. Blot the stain with turpentine. Test first for colorfastness. Blot repeatedly, alternating turpentine and clean water, until most of the stain is removed.

3. Sponge well with clean water.

4. If the stain remains, sponge with dry-cleaning fluid and blot continuously.

5. Sponge a lukewarm sudsy laundry detergent mixture onto the stain and blot until no more stain can be removed.

6. Sponge well with clean water and let carpet dry
    thoroughly.

7. Vacuum.

---

69. **RUST**

General
Description:

*The reddish brittle coating formed on iron and other
metals, especially when chemically attacked by moist air,
and composed essentially of hydrated ferric oxide.* Though
rust weakens metal objects, making them more pliable,
it actually increases the weight of the article—for example, one ton of iron turns into three tons of rust. Rust is
an inevitable result of metal meeting the outdoor elements. This means that there is the potential for a rust
stain from just about anywhere: metal stadium seats,
metal pipes, the monkey bars on a playground, random
gadgets and tools in the garage or basement, and any
exposed metal on an old automobile.

Season:

In moderate climates, rust stains develop at all times of
the year, as the weather takes its toll on any unprotected
metallic surface. In climates where rain is limited there
is less rust-stain potential—you are less likely to
encounter rust in the desert than in a tropical climate.

Areas of
Occurrence:

Although rust stains can present themselves in any
number of places, they are likely to appear on sweat-

shirts, sweatpants, jeans, and other clothes you might wear when working with plumbing, under the hood of a car, cleaning out the garage, or visiting a stadium with metal seats.

Time of Occurrence:
Rust stains are almost always met with a look of surprise from their victims—most people don't think to check under a metal seat before sliding a coat underneath it, and they may not think about the potential for contracting a rust stain when changing a tire. The surprise of finding a rust stain, then, could happen at any time of day.

REMOVAL:

1. Apply a mild bleach, such as lemon juice, to the stain, then sprinkle with salt to absorb it. For colored fabrics, test first for colorfastness.

2. Let fabric sit in direct sunlight. The sun will help to bleach the stain. Test first for colorfastness.

3. Continue to apply lemon juice and salt until the stain is removed. Do not let the stain dry between applications.

 4. Rinse well in warm water.

 5. Launder according to garment label.

6. If the stain remains, treat with a rust remover according to manufacturer's directions.

70.   **SCORCH MARKS**

General
Description:
Marks caused by slight burning; usually gray or black in color. Scorch marks are extremely common from cooking, camping, ironing, or smoking, and are a particularly pesky stain to remove. Oddly enough, a part of clothing or fabric that has already burned cannot be burned again.

Season:

Since cooking is a year-round activity, scorch marks resulting from this activity will not be limited to any time of year: likewise, the gray stains resulting from smoking or ironing. Camping, however, is generally a spring and summer activity, and so stains that happen 'round the campfire are limited to those months.

Areas of
Occurrence:

The most common spot for this stain on clothing is the sleeves of a turtleneck, sweatshirt, sweater, or coat. However, the errant ash could find its way onto the fronts of these garments as well, and is even a possibility on trouser legs.

Time of
Occurrence:
A high-risk period is when you smoke or tend a blaze late at night; scorch marks are more prevalent during darkness as well as—perhaps—the consumption of spirits.

REMOVAL: *On light fabric:*

1. Brush off or shake scorched area gently to remove charring.

2. Dampen a piece of white cotton with diluted hydrogen peroxide (at a ratio of 1 part hydrogen peroxide, 4 parts water) and sponge the scorch mark.

3. Let garment dry in the sun for added bleaching.

4. Repeat sponging and drying until no more stain can be removed.

5. Sponge one last time with the peroxide mixture.

6. Cover the mark with a clean, dry, absorbent cloth.

7. Press a medium-warm iron over the cloth. Replace the cloth as the peroxide soaks through. Do not let the iron come into contact with the fabric, since the peroxide can cause rust to form. (If this happens, see RUST on page 153.)

8. If scorch mark remains, repeat steps 2 through 7 until you've removed as much of the scorch mark as possible.

9. Rinse in warm water.

10. Apply a laundry presoak (spot stain remover) and let stand several minutes.

11. Launder according to garment label.

12. If the stain remains, launder with an all-fabric bleach. Test first for colorfastness.

On wool:

1. Sponge the stain with diluted hydrogen peroxide as in step 2 above.

2. Wash in warm water with a little borax powder.

3. Rinse well and air dry.

4. If the stain remains, brush it with an emery board.

---

71. **SHOE POLISH**

General Description:

A substance used to give smoothness or gloss to an external covering for the human foot. Shoe polish is a necessity for any style-conscious person, but its uses don't end with the feet. It's a must-have for children at Halloween, or any time you need to darken your face or hands and no makeup is available. Popular colors include black, brown, blue, and white.

Season:

Shoe polish stains are year-round occurrences, but the colors vary with the time of year. White shoe-polish stains are only incurred in the summer, as long as style guidelines are followed to the letter. Brown and black shoe-polish stains should only occur in the colder months. Additionally, as noted above, October 31 will see an increase in shoe-polish stains of every color.

Areas of
Occurrence:

Pant-leg and dress-shirt cuffs are the areas most affected by this stain. Suit jackets can be marred when the polisher is hurried. In rare instances, pantyhose, socks, and tights may also fall victim to this stain.

Time of
Occurrence:

In train and bus stations around the world, busy commuters get their shoes polished before or after work; therefore, morning and evening rush hours are common times to obtain this stain. Costume parties are also a time to look out for the shoe-polish stain.

REMOVAL:

1. Use a dull knife or spoon to remove as much as possible.

2. Rinse back of stain with cold water, then rub with a bar soap, dishwashing liquid, or liquid laundry detergent. Rub the stain between thumbs.

3. Rinse well.

4. Repeat steps 2 and 3 until no more stain can be removed.

5. If the stain remains, rub with detergent, then soak garment in water for 10 to 15 minutes.

6. Rinse well.

 7. If the stain remains, treat with a laundry presoak (spot stain remover) and let stand several minutes.

 8. Launder according to garment label.

72. **SOOT OR SMOKE**

General Description:

Soot: *A black substance formed by combustion or separated from fuel during combustion, rising in fine particles and adhering to the sides of the chimney or pipe conveying the smoke; especially the fine powder consisting chiefly of carbon that colors smoke.* Smoke: *The gaseous products of burning carbonaceous materials made visible by the presence of small particles of carbon.* A perfectly clean fire produces almost no smoke. Smoke means that a fire is not burning properly and that bits of unburned material are escaping. Unfortunately, this perfect fire is uncommon, and smoke, soot, and ash—and their various stains—are present in most (if not all) the fires we encounter. Producing smoke and soot is also a part of the daily rituals of more than 48 million smokers worldwide.

Season:

Because cigarette smoking is an addiction, it isn't limited to season—stains from cigarettes can be gotten at any time of year, in smokers' homes or cars (road trips can be especially grueling), at all-night diners, and especially in seedy bars. Soot and ash stainings are likely in the fall, winter, and spring, when you are most likely to clean a fireplace; but the same stains are just as likely in summer from campfires and pit barbecues.

Areas of Occurrence:

Soot and ash fly through the air, landing on furniture, carpets, and all imaginable articles of clothing. Purses and bags are not immune to these stains, either. Obviously, the uniforms of firefighters are exposed to these stains—from the top of the hat to the bottom of the boot.

Time of Occurrence:

Smoke, soot, and ash are not limited by time of day— heavy smokers indulge their addiction regardless of the hour. If you are a nonsmoker, nighttime activities such as drinking alcohol or lighting campfires increase the chance for acquiring a stain.

REMOVAL: *If the fabric is washable:*

1. Take the fabric outside and gently shake or brush off as much soot as possible. If possible, hold the garment taut and vacuum the stain.

2. Sprinkle an absorbent powder, such as talcum powder, baking soda, or salt, on the stain and let stand for several minutes.

3. Brush off outdoors or vacuum.

4. Repeat steps 2 and 3 until you have removed as much as possible.

5. Apply laundry presoak (spot stain remover) and let stand several minutes.

6. Launder in the hottest water safe for the fabric. For extra-heavy stains, replace half the amount of detergent with baking soda.

If the fabric is not washable:

1. Take the fabric outside and gently shake or brush off as much soot as possible. If possible, hold the garment taut and vacuum the stain.

2. Sponge the stain with dry-cleaning fluid according to manufacturer's directions.

3. Air out as much residual odor as possible by hanging the garment outside or at least out of the closet for a few days.

On carpet:

1. Vacuum loose particles.

2. **Sprinkle stain with salt and let stand 1 to 2 hours.**

3. **Vacuum.**

4. **Repeat steps 2 and 3 until you have removed as much stain as possible.**

5. **Apply a carpet spotter according to manufacturer's directions.**

---

73. 📷 **TARNISH**

General Description:
The film that dulls the luster of or discolors a metallic surface, especially caused by oxidation. Tarnish can leave an ugly black stain on clothing, and can ruin pots and pans in your kitchen, not to mention silverware and silver pieces in your home. A simple home remedy for cleaning the tarnished bottoms of pots and pans is to spread a little ketchup on the affected surface, and let it sit for about one minute. Wipe clean and rinse, and they're good as new!

Season:
Since pots, lamps, and other metallic items tarnish with age, there isn't be a particular season when more of this staining happens.

Areas of Occurrence:
The sleeves of any clothing worn when cleaning or cooking are vulnerable to this stain, as well as the fronts

of these garments. The legs and seat of an old pair of jeans might well be affected, since tarnish transfers easily to hands, which are often wiped carelessly on clothing. This is especially common when polishing silver jewelry or flatware.

Time of
Occurrence:

Because cleaning is an anytime activity, stains encountered when polishing a lamp will not be limited to a specific time of day. Tarnish stains are also frequently incurred during the course of cooking a meal.

REMOVAL:

1. Place garment on an absorbent cloth. Sponge the stain with a mild bleach, such as hydrogen peroxide, white vinegar, or lemon juice. Test first for colorfastness. Replace cloth as it becomes saturated.

2. Rinse thoroughly.

3. Repeat steps 1 and 2 until you have removed as much stain as possible.

4. Launder according to garment label.

74. **TOBACCO**

General
Description:

Any plant of the genus Nicotiana, *of the nightshade family, especially any of the species whose leaves are prepared for smoking or chewing, or as snuff.* Tobacco is probably the oldest addictive drug in existence. It comes in many forms and flavors for smoking and chewing pleasure. Smoking itself has a lore all its own—for example the superstition in the British army that to light three cigarettes on the same match is bad luck. This comes from the Boer War (1899–1902), when the flame would give the enemy sniper time to sight his rifle, and the soldier with the third cigarette was invariably shot.

Season:

Serious smokers light up every day, so these stains aren't confined to particular months. Chewing tobacco may more frequently stain during the summer baseball season, since a mouthful of chew is a staple of America's pastime. Tobacco from cigars may more often stain during celebrations, such as for the birth of a baby, but these, too, occur throughout the year.

Areas of
Occurrence:

When rolling your own cigarettes, tobacco is likely to stain the lap areas of jeans and slacks, as well as the fronts of jackets and sweaters. Chewing tobacco is a more far-reaching stain because it involves spitting, so don't be surprised if this brown stain mars shoes, socks, pant legs, and even carpets should you choose to chew.

Time of
Occurrence:

Tobacco stains are most likely to occur after dark, in dimly lit bars or restaurants, though they won't be limited to this time; most smokers enjoy their tobacco throughout the day.

Variations of
Significance:

Chewing tobacco; cigarettes; cigars

REMOVAL:

1. Brush off excess material outdoors.

2. Use a dull knife or spoon to remove as much as possible.

 3. Rinse the back of the stain well with cold water.

4. Blot with an absorbent cloth.

 5. Treat with a laundry presoak (spot stain remover) and let stand 20 to 30 minutes. For tough stains, first rub with glycerin and let stand until the stain is softened, then apply a laundry presoak.

6. Launder according to garment label.

75.   **WATER SPOTS**

General
Description:

Spots left by water on delicate fabrics such as silk, rayon, or fine wool. It may take 120 drops of water to fill a tea-spoon, but it only takes one errant drop to damage a fine silk blouse. Water is usually the substance you use to remove stains, thus it seems paradoxical to concern ourselves with removing stains incurred by this very agent. Water spots are the result of a garment being splashed and the drops drying slowly over time, leaving a telltale ring of deposits.

Season:

The period of highest risk for developing water spots is during the seasons when weather is most active—in moderate climates, usually winter and spring. There is some chance of finding these spots year round, especially for those who are very concerned about their outward appearance and use steam irons to smooth wrinkles in their clothes.

Areas of
Occurrence:

Water spots can present themselves anywhere on a garment if acquired through ironing. If acquired during a rain or snow storm, the fronts and backs of shirts, pants, dresses, sweaters, coats, and jackets are most at risk, and the arms and shoulders of these garments will almost certainly need to be treated.

REMOVAL: *On silk, rayon, or wool:*

1. Fill a kettle with water and bring to a boil. Cover the spout with cheesecloth to prevent water droplets from splattering out.

2. Once the water is boiling, hold the stained fabric over the steam until it becomes damp, but not wet.

3. Shake and press the fabric while it is still damp. Rub the affected area with a spoon or other dull surface.

On carpet:

1. Blot as much of the spill as possible. Lay absorbent cloths over the stain and walk on them to absorb excess liquid.

2. Dry the stain as quickly as possible by covering the spill with sheets of absorbent material, such as paper towels or blotting paper. Stack books on top of the absorbent sheets. Point a fan at the spill. (Never use a radiator as the heat can cause some carpet to scorch and shrink.) As the water dries, it will be forced up into the sheets. Replace the sheets as they become saturated.

or

If possible, prop the carpet up and aim a fan at the stain to dry both sides (top and bottom). If you can

take the carpet up, it is recommended that you
have a professional reinstall and steam-clean it.

---

76. **WAX, CANDLE**

General
Description:

*A solid, yellowish, non-glycerine substance allied to fats
and oils, secreted by bees in constructing their honeycomb,
molded, embedded with a wick, often scented and dyed,
and lit by humans to provide light and/or aroma.* Though
candles functioned at one time as a strictly utilitarian
device, they have now become synonymous with
romance and good decorating.

Season:

Candles are burned throughout the year for their warm
glow and pleasing scents at romantic dinners and parties
alike. There is perhaps an increase in candle stains during Hanukkah, when the menorah burns for eight days,
and at birthday parties, especially when the guest of
honor is of advanced years, requiring more candles.

Areas of
Occurrence:

Dripping wax can be quite far-reaching, especially when
the candle itself is being blown out. Too forceful an
exhalation and the hot wax will splatter everywhere; it
can stain evening gowns, tuxedos, sweaters, and jeans as
well as wallpaper, carpets, tables, and curtains.

Time of
Occurrence:

The most common time for a wax stain to develop is
after dark, when romance is in the air.

Variations of
Significance: Birthday cakes; lanterns; menorahs

REMOVAL: *On fabric:*

1. Put an ice cube in a plastic bag and rub the wax
    until it is brittle, or place the entire garment in the
    freezer. Peel off as much wax as possible.

2. If a residue remains, lay an absorbent cloth or
    unprinted side of a brown paper bag over the stain.

 3. Gently press the cloth with a warm iron. The wax
    will melt and seep into the cloth. If the cloth
    begins to brown, replace with a fresh cloth.
    Continue to iron until the wax has been com-
    pletely absorbed by the cloth.

4. If the candle is colored and the wax has left a dye
    stain, blot it with rubbing alcohol.

 5. If the stain remains, apply a laundry presoak (spot
    stain remover) and let stand several minutes.

 6. Launder according to garment label.

On hard surfaces, such as wood, tiles, or paneling:

1. Put an ice cube in a plastic bag and rub the wax

until it is brittle. Peel off as much wax as possible.

2. If a residue remains, lay an absorbent cloth or unprinted side of a brown paper bag over the stain.

 3. Gently press the cloth with a warm iron. The wax will melt and seep into the cloth. If the cloth begins to brown, replace with a fresh cloth. Continue to iron until the wax has been completely absorbed by the cloth.

4. If a dye stain remains, wipe with rubbing alcohol. Rinse surface with water.

77. **YELLOWING**

General
Description:

The process by which fabrics turn yellow after a period of time. Some yellowed clothing may inspire a wave of nostalgia—a Christening gown, a wedding dress, a prom dress, a military uniform, or a graduation gown. After the wedding, many brides opt to seal their gowns to protect them from signs of aging and other damaging threats. However, sealing a gown can actually accelerate the aging process, because condensation forms inside the bag and often results in yellowing.

Season:

Yellowing occurs over a period of time, so there is no season during which you can be more vigilant to prevent it. You are most likely to *discover* the yellowing during spring cleaning, around anniversaries when nostalgia requires a peek into the past, and the dead of winter, when cabin fever causes many to resort to cleaning out closets for entertainment.

Areas of Occurrence: Yellowing can affect an entire garment—it does not discriminate.

REMOVAL:

1. Fill a bucket with warm water and add denture-cleaning tablets according to manufacturer's directions.

2. Once the tablets are dissolved, add stained garment and soak until the yellowing is gone.

3. Rinse well.

 4. Launder according to garment label.

Garage and Yard

  CHARCOAL

General
Description:
The carbonaceous material obtained by heating an organic substance, like wood, in the absence of air. A necessity at any barbecue that doesn't involve a gas or electric grill, charcoal briquettes were invented by Henry Ford. While barbecues are the most obvious and common use for charcoal, it can also be used to create artistic master-pieces, or to darken the eyes at Halloween or other festive times when costumes or disguises are called for.

Season:
Summer is prime time for charcoal stains, since it's the best time for barbecues on the hibachi. Charcoal is used in artwork year-round, so stains from this are not con-fined to any particular time of year.

Areas of
Occurrence:
Since charcoal smudges as often as it doesn't, its stains can be far-reaching. The front of your apron or smock is a prime target, as are the sleeves of your T-shirt or sweater. Since hands readily acquire charcoal, and the legs and seats of jeans and trousers are the easiest places to wipe hands clean, these areas of clothing often show charcoal stains.

REMOVAL:
1. Take the fabric outside and gently shake or brush off as much charcoal as possible. If possible, hold

the garment taut and vacuum the stain.

 2. Sprinkle an absorbent powder, such as talcum powder, baking soda, or salt, on the stain and let stand for several minutes.

 3. Brush off outdoors or vacuum.

4. Repeat steps 2 and 3 until you have removed as much stain as possible.

 5. Rinse the back of the stain with warm water.

 6. Apply laundry presoak (spot stain remover) and let stand several minutes.

 7. Launder in the hottest water safe for the fabric. For extra-heavy stains, replace half the amount of detergent with baking soda.

---

79. **DIRT OR MUD**

General Description:
Dirt: *Specifically, the portion of the earth's surface consisting of disintegrated rock and humus; generally, any foul or filthy substance, as mud, grime, or dust.* Mud: *wet, soft earth or earthy matter, as on the ground after rain, at the bottom of a pond, or along the banks of a river; mire.* An unusual eating disorder called *tomatophagia* (also

known as pica) is blamed on iron deficiency anemia. People with *tomatophagia* develop unusual cravings for such things as tomatoes, ice, detergent, starch, clay, or even dirt. Those who actually give in to these cravings not only open themselves up to sickness but to some nasty stain possibilities.

Season:

There is no escaping the ubiquitous staining, since every season has its own type of dirt or mud. Winter brings mud from melting snow, from slush on the roads and sidewalks, or from sleds gone astray. Spring brings mud from even more melted snow, from tilling the garden, from playing baseball, softball, and soccer. Summer brings dust storms, dirt kicked up from bike tires, and mud from picking vegetables in the garden, from swimming in lakes and creeks, and from children's mudpies prepared in the backyard. Fall brings the dirt and mud of a wet football field, of raking the leaves in the yard, and of camping and hiking.

Area of
Occurrence:

Stains from dirt and mud can coat any area of the body, especially shoes, socks, and the cuffs of pants. Mud from a roadside can splash all over your best dress, slacks, or jacket; a muddy sports field can coat a uniform with half the field by the end of a game. And carpets are perhaps the most vulnerable of all possible surfaces to a dirt or mud stain.

Time of
Occurrence:

There is no time of day or night when dirt and mud
are not stain hazards.

Variations of
Significance:

Houseplant soil

REMOVAL: *If the fabric is washable:*

1. Let stain dry completely. Do not smear or wipe it
   while wet; this will only set and spread the stain.

2. Once dry, shake the stain to remove as much dirt
   as possible. Or vacuum the fabric.

3. Rub liquid enzyme detergent into the stain, then
   soak in water for 10 to 20 minutes or until the
   stain is gone. Rub the stain between thumbs occasionally during soaking. Older stains may need to
   be soaked for several hours.

4. If the stain remains, apply a laundry presoak (spot
   stain remover) and let stand several minutes.

5. Launder with enzyme detergent.

6. If the stain remains, repeat step 3.

7. Blot remaining color stain with white vinegar or
   hydrogen peroxide.

8. Rinse well.

 9. Launder according to garment label.

If the fabric is not washable:

1. Let stain dry completely. Do not smear or wipe it while wet.

 2. Once dry, shake the stain to remove as much dirt as possible. Or vacuum the fabric.

3. Mix a sudsy solution of liquid enzyme detergent and water, and sponge mixture onto stain.

 4. Rinse stained area with water.

5. Repeat as needed.

On carpet:

 1. Sprinkle stain with salt, baking soda, or other absorbent powder and let dry.

 2. Vacuum.

3. Repeat until you have removed as much stain as possible.

4. **Treat with a carpet spotter according to manufacturer's directions.**

80. **GASOLINE**

General
Description:

A volatile, flammable liquid mixture of hydrocarbons obtained from petroleum and used chiefly as fuel for internal-combustion engines. With its unmistakable smell and myriad uses, gasoline is easily the most popular fuel around—your car or boat couldn't live without it. Gasoline does not burn; rather, it emits gasses that burn. Due to cleaner burning gasoline and improved technology, today it takes about 26 new cars to produce the tailpipe pollution of one new car in the 1960s.

Season:

Filling up the tank of your SUV or sports car is a year-round activity, but you'll usually fill your speedboat with gas in the summertime, making this stain slightly more probable during the warmer months.

Areas of
Occurrence:

It is illegal to pump your own gas in the states of New Jersey and Oregon; therefore, the motorists in those states are virtually immune to this stinky stain. Running out of gas on the side of the road can happen anywhere, however, and cans of gasoline are unwieldy. When using a gas can, as when using a gas pump, you are bound to occasionally splash the liquid onto shoes, socks, or the cuffs of trousers.

Time of
Occurrence: A gas station attendant or motorist may encounter this
               stain any time of day or night, as thoughtful proprietors
               know that fuel is always needed, and many stations are
               open 24 hours a day.

REMOVAL: *On fabric:*

1. Use a dull knife or spoon to remove as much as
   possible.

2. Blot remaining liquid with an absorbent cloth.

 3. Sprinkle salt, baking soda, cornstarch, or talcum
   powder on stain to absorb excess liquid, let stand
   10 to 15 minutes, then brush off.

4. Rub colorless dishwashing liquid into the stain. Let
   stand 1 to 2 minutes.

5. Soak in a sudsy mixture of hot water and dishwashing liquid for up to 30 minutes.

 6. Rinse the back of the stain well with hot water.

7. Use a dull knife or spoon to remove any loosened
   grease or oil from the fabric.

8. If the stain remains, repeat steps 3 through 7.

9. If the stain remains, make a paste of baking soda and water at a ratio of approximately 3 to 1, spread on the stain and let dry, then brush off.

10. Apply laundry presoak (spot stain remover) and let stand several minutes.

11. Launder in the hottest water safe for the fabric. For extra-heavy stains, replace half the amount of detergent with baking soda.

12. If the stain remains, repeat steps 2 through 7.

On carpet:

1. Use a dull knife or spoon to remove as much as possible.

2. Blot remaining liquid with an absorbent cloth. (For heavy or dark stains, it is best to call a professional cleaner.)

3. Sprinkle the stain with an absorbent powder, such as baking soda, cornstarch, cornmeal, or talcum powder. Let sit for 6 to 12 hours, then vacuum (do not brush) the powder.

or

Spray with shaving cream and work it into the carpet with an old toothbrush. Wipe with a damp cloth, then sponge with cold water.

or

Dampen with club soda and blot. Repeat as needed.

4. If the stain remains, apply dry-cleaning fluid (be careful not to wet the carpet backing with it), then sponge the stain with a damp cloth.

or

Treat with a carpet spotter according to manufacturer's directions.

---

81.   **GRASS**

General
Description:

Any of a large family (Gramineae) *of mostly herbaceous plants with narrow leaves, jointed stems, and spikes or clusters of minute flowers—commonly found behind, between, and in front of homes, apartment buildings, and in other public spaces, such as recreational areas and on college campuses.* Nearly unavoidable during times of moderate weather, this plant is frequently the object of obsession for many (especially suburban) men and women. Grass grows quickly when watered, hence, many people regularly trim it to a comfortable height of, on average, about three inches.

Season:

Grass stains appear during periods of moderate weather when you are likely to be spending time outdoors—spring, summer, and fall are the seasons when you are most likely to roll down hills, sit in the park, or go camping. Grass stains rarely appear in winter, except during an occasional particularly bad spill from a sled, or in areas where the climate is moderate year-round.

Areas of Occurrence:

The most obvious spots for grass stains are the seats and knees of pants, the seats of skirts and shorts, and the elbows of jackets and long-sleeved shirts, depending on how comfortable the wearers become in the grass. In a logroll competition, no clothing is safe from the grass stain. Baseball, softball, and soccer players acquire grass stains on all areas of their uniforms, especially when sliding to base or defending the goal. When mowing the grass be particularly conscious of the cuffs of pant legs.

Time of Occurrence:

Since picnics in the park and other recreational activities take place throughout the year, especially in the warm summer months, this stubborn stain is not limited by time. Stains acquired while mowing the lawn probably occur most often in the early morning, a favorite time of day for this activity.

Variations of Significance:

Floral arrangements; golf greens; mulch from grass clippings

REMOVAL:

1. **Place garment stain-side down on absorbent cloth and sponge back of stain with rubbing alcohol, replacing pad underneath as needed. Test first for colorfastness. (For acetate fabrics, dilute alcohol**

with 2 parts water. Do not use alcohol on wool.)

2. Rinse well in cold water.

3. If the stain remains, use an old toothbrush to scrub the stain with non-gel toothpaste (preferably containing baking soda). Let stand for 2 to 3 minutes. If toothpaste is not available, sponge the stain with white vinegar.

4. Rinse well.

5. If the stain remains, repeat steps 1 through 4 until you've removed as much stain as possible.

6. Rub the stain with laundry presoak (spot stain remover) and let stand for several minutes.

7. Launder with a liquid enzyme detergent.

Very heavy, stubborn, remaining stains can also be treated as a DYES OR RUNNING COLORS stain. See page 127.

82. 📷 **GREASE**

General
Description:

Fatty or oily matter in general; lubricant. In 1400 B.C. affluent Egyptian women wore cones of scented grease on top of their heads. As the day wore on, the hot sun would melt the grease, causing it to drip down their bodies, covering their skin with a glistening sheen, and saturating their clothes with fragrance. In contemporary times, grease is more likely to be used as a lubricant in cars and other mechanical devices than as a vehicle for fragrance.

Season:

Grease stains can present themselves at any time, especially if you are mechanically inclined, work around lots of moving parts, or have the nickname "grease monkey."

Areas of
Occurrence:

People who work around cars and other machines that employ grease as a lubricant often have special clothes, like jumpsuits or coveralls, to protect other pieces of clothing from damaging stains. These protective garments are of course vulnerable to staining in any location. People who do not work around grease are not immune, however—the edges of car doors are notorious for preying on the clothing of an unsuspecting victim, especially in the arm or buttocks region. Bicycle riders should also beware, as grease from the chain can easily stain socks and pants cuffs.

| Variations of Significance: | Bicycle chains; car doors; greased hinges |

REMOVAL: *On fabric:*

1. Use a dull knife or spoon to remove as much as possible.

2. Blot remaining liquid with an absorbent cloth.

 3. Sprinkle salt, baking soda, cornstarch, or talcum powder on stain to absorb excess grease and let stand 15 to 30 minutes, then brush off. Repeat until you have removed as much stain as possible.

4. Rub colorless dishwashing liquid into stain. Let stand 1 to 2 minutes.

5. Soak in hot water for up to 30 minutes.

 6. Rinse the back of the stain well with hot water.

7. Use a dull knife or spoon again to remove any loosened grease from the fabric.

8. Blot with an absorbent cloth.

9. If the stain remains, make a paste of baking soda and water at a ratio of approximately 3 to 1, spread

on stain and let dry, then brush off.

10. Apply laundry presoak (spot stain remover) and let stand several minutes.

11. Launder in the hottest water safe for the fabric. For extra-heavy stains, replace half the amount of detergent with baking soda.

12. If the stain remains, repeat steps 3 through 11.

On carpet:

1. Use a dull knife or spoon to remove as much as possible.

2. Blot remaining liquid with an absorbent cloth. (For heavy or dark stains, it is best to call a professional cleaner.)

3. Sprinkle the stain with an absorbent powder, such as baking soda, cornstarch, cornmeal, or talcum powder. Let sit for 6 to 12 hours, then vacuum (do not brush) the powder.

or

Spray with shaving cream and work it into the carpet with an old toothbrush. Wipe it off with a damp cloth, then sponge with cold water.

or

Dampen with club soda and blot. Repeat as needed.

4. If the stain remains, apply dry-cleaning fluid (be careful not to wet the carpet backing with it), then sponge the stain with a damp cloth.

or

Treat with a carpet spotter according to manufacturer's directions.

On wallpaper or walls:

1. Make a paste of cornstarch or baking soda and water at a ratio of approximately 3 to 1, then smear the paste onto stain. Non-gel toothpaste can also be used. Let paste dry, then wipe with a clean cloth. For toothpaste, let stand 10 to 15 minutes, then wipe with a damp cloth.

2. Repeat until the stain is gone.

---

83. **OIL, MOTOR**

General
Description:

A thick, viscous, combustible liquid of refined petroleum, used in the maintenance of automobiles and other moving machinery. Bottled motor oil, which is available at most filling stations and garages, allows more and more people to add and change their own oil, so this stain is not limited to mechanics and gas station attendants.

However, car enthusiasts and professionals alike should take care with this dark, sticky substance, as it is extremely toxic. A mere quart of motor oil can pollute 250,000 gallons of water.

Season: Since oil changes are supposed to be done every several thousand miles or every few months (whichever comes first), stains from the process are not more prevalent in a particular season. Motor oil will stain throughout the year.

Areas of Occurrence: Depending on how they are obtained, motor oil stains can appear anywhere on your person. After a long day at the garage, mechanics may look as though they have bathed in the stuff, finding it all over the sleeves, legs, fronts, and backs of their jumpsuits, not to mention on skin, hair, and in ears. The backs of shirts, sweaters, pants, and jackets are particularly susceptible when you are lying down in a driveway, under a car. If you trip in a parking lot on a hot day, motor oil stains are likely to show up on the knees and/or seat of your jeans or slacks.

Time of Occurrence: A garage attendant, mechanic, or motorist can obtain this stain any time of day or night, as oil changes or additions are not limited to daytime, and many stations are open 24-hours. After a particularly messy day, a mechanic or automobile enthusiast may even transfer these nasty stains to carpets or walls upon returning home.

REMOVAL: *On fabric:*

1. Use a dull knife or spoon to remove as much as possible.

2. Blot remaining liquid with an absorbent cloth.

 3. Sprinkle salt, baking soda, cornstarch, or talcum powder on stain to absorb excess oil, let stand 10 to 15 minutes, then brush off.

4. Rub colorless dishwashing liquid into stain. Let stand 1 to 2 minutes.

5. Soak in a sudsy mixture of hot water and dishwashing liquid for up to 30 minutes.

 6. Rinse the back of the stain well with hot water.

7. Use a dull knife or spoon to remove any loosened oil from the fabric.

8. If the stain remains, make a paste of baking soda and water at a ratio of approximately 3 to 1, spread on stain and let dry, then brush off.

 9. Apply laundry presoak (spot stain remover) and let stand several minutes to penetrate fabric.

10. Launder in the hottest water safe for the fabric. For extra-heavy stains, replace half the amount of detergent with baking soda.

11. If the stain remains, repeat steps 3 through 10.

On carpet:

1. Use a dull knife or spoon to remove as much as possible.

2. Blot remaining liquid with an absorbent cloth. (For heavy or dark stains, it is best to call a professional cleaner.)

3. Sprinkle the stain with an absorbent powder such as baking soda, cornstarch, cornmeal, or talcum powder. Let sit for 6 to 12 hours, then vacuum (do not brush) the powder.

or

Spray with shaving cream and work it into the carpet with an old toothbrush. Wipe it off with a damp cloth, then sponge with cold water.

or

Dampen with club soda and blot. Repeat as needed.

4. If the stain remains, apply dry-cleaning fluid (be careful not to wet the carpet backing with it), then sponge the stain with a damp cloth.

or

Treat with a carpet spotter according to manufacturer's directions.

On wallpaper or walls:

1. Make a paste of baking soda and water at a ratio of approximately 3 to 1, then smear the paste onto stain. Non-gel toothpaste can also be used. Let paste dry, then wipe off. For toothpaste, let stand 10 to 15 minutes, then wipe off with a damp cloth.

2. Repeat until the stain is gone.

---

84. **POLLEN**

General Description:

The fertilizing element of flowering plants, consisting of fine, powdery, yellowish grains or spores, sometimes in masses. Most plant pollen is highly flammable, exploding when placed on an extremely hot surface. In the early days of modern theater, artificial lightning was produced by throwing pollen grains onto a hot shovel. These days, you are more likely to encounter pollen outdoors, in its natural element, than backstage or on a movie set.

Season:

Hay-fever sufferers know that pollen is in season during the spring, summer, and winter months in most climates. You may acquire pollen stains when working in the garden or tending to fresh flowers. Pay attention to those beautiful lilies in early spring, with their huge stamens quivering with pollen, ready to inflict a bright yellow spot on your finest spring attire. Pollen has become popular as a source of natural vitamins and minerals, increasing the chances for year-round staining.

Areas of Occurrence:

Pollen can stain pant legs and skirts as you wander through the garden or across a field of goldenrod. Pollen can also color the sleeves and fronts of shirts, particularly when you are flower arranging. In early summer, trees drop pollen all over streets and cars, making this stain nearly impossible to avoid, as it shows up on shoes, socks, and even jackets and pants.

REMOVAL:

1. Shake garment outdoors to remove loose pollen.

2. Use a dull knife or spoon to remove as much as possible.

3. Rinse the back of the stain well with cold water.

4. Soak garment in cold water until the stain is loosened.

5. Rinse well.

6. Repeat steps 3 through 5 until you have removed

as much stain as possible.

 7. If the stain remains, apply a laundry presoak (spot stain remover) and let stand several minutes.

 8. Launder in the hottest water safe for the fabric.

---

85. **SAP**

General
Description:

A watery juice, containing mineral salts and sugar, that circulates through the tissues of plants. Sugar-maple tree sap is the basic ingredient for tasty maple syrup, but this fluid is not limited to maple syrup production. Sap has medicinal uses as well: South American tree sap is a painkiller, anti-inflammatory, and antibiotic.

Season:

Because the sap used to make maple syrup is generally collected in autumn, an increase in sap stains at that time of year is to be expected. However, since plants and trees release sap year-round, tree huggers, tree surgeons, and loggers, as well as gardeners and nursery workers, must be vigilant throughout the year.

Areas of
Occurrence:

If you operate on or climb a tree, the legs of your jeans and trousers most certainly are vulnerable to this stain. The cuffs, sleeves, and fronts of jackets and sweaters are also prime targets. Plant sap also finds its way onto gardening gloves, smocks, and sweatshirts. While sap is being collected for maple syrup or medicinal purposes, shoes, socks, boots, and the legs of pants are all common stain areas.

Time of
Occurrence:
Most stains from this sticky liquid are experienced during daylight hours, when tree surgeries and sap-collecting most often take place.

REMOVAL:
1. Use a dull knife or spoon to remove as much as possible.

2. Rub glycerin into the stain and let stand several minutes until sap is softened. For old stains, warm the glycerin, spread it over the stain, and let stand.

3. Place stain over an absorbent cloth and tap the back of it with an old toothbrush to loosen the stain. Replace the cloth as it becomes saturated. Continue until you have removed as much as possible.

4. If a color stain remains, apply a laundry presoak (spot stain remover) and let stand several minutes.

5. Launder according to garment label.

86. **TAR OR ASPHALT**

General
Description:

Tar: *Any of various dark-colored, viscid products obtained by the destructive distillation of certain organic substances, such as coal or wood.* Asphalt: *Any of various dark-colored, solid, bituminous substances, native in various areas of the earth and composed mainly of hydrocarbon mixtures; a mixture of such substances with gravel, crushed rock, or the like, used for paving.* Asphalt is the preferred substance for paving streets because it is less expensive than concrete, and because, unlike concrete, it is flexible. When water freezing underground causes the earth to expand, an asphalt-paved road will expand with it, while a concrete-paved road will crack.

Season:

For the general public, tar and asphalt stains occur almost exclusively during the warm months of late spring, summer, and early fall. These substances are solid when they're cold, so there is little risk of them spreading and smearing during the winter months. However, construction workers may be susceptible to the stains year-round, when roofing, filling potholes, or paving new roads.

Area of
Occurrence:

Tar and asphalt stick readily to shoes, socks, and cuffs of pants. Stains on knees and elbows are also possible, especially following spills from bikes, skateboards, Roller Blades, and other forms of locomotion.

REMOVAL: *On fabric:*

1. Rub the affected area with ice, then use a dull knife or spoon to remove as much as possible.

2. Rub glycerin into the stain and lay stained area over an absorbent cloth. (If tar has dried, warm the glycerin first, then spread it over the stain.)

3. When the stain is softened, tap the back of it with an old toothbrush or spoon to remove as much tar as possible. Replace the cloth as necessary.

4. Rub eucalyptus oil or turpentine into the remaining stain and blot. Continue until you have removed as much stain as possible.

5. Apply laundry presoak (spot stain remover) and let stand several minutes.

6. Launder according to garment label.

7. If the stain remains, rub liquid laundry detergent into the stain and rub it between your thumbs.

8. Rinse well in hot water.

9. Repeat steps 7 and 8 until you have removed as much stain as possible.

10. If the stain remains, apply a laundry presoak (spot stain remover) and let stand several minutes.

11. Launder in the hottest water safe for the fabric.

12. If the stain remains, lay garment in the sun and sponge with a mild bleach, such as hydrogen peroxide. Keep stain moist.

13. Rinse well.

On carpet:

1. Rub the affected area with ice, then use a dull knife or spoon to remove as much as possible. If tar is dried, rub warm glycerin into it and let it soak until the tar or asphalt is softened.

2. Blot stain gently with an absorbent cloth to remove as much tar and asphalt as possible. Replace cloth as it becomes covered with the stain. Continue until you have removed as much stain as possible.

3. Sponge the stain with eucalyptus oil or turpentine, blotting continuously.

4. Sponge the stain with a sudsy detergent solution, then scrub with an old toothbrush to work solution into carpet.

5. Blot with water to rinse.

6. If the stain remains, apply dry-cleaning fluid or a carpet spotter according to manufacturer's directions.

---

87. **WINDSHIELD WIPER FLUID**

General Description:
A blue liquid stored in a container under an automobile's hood, which is shot onto the glass that stretches across the front of the vehicle, and then is wiped off to clean the glass and increase visibility. Although water can be used in place of windshield wiper fluid in warm weather, the blue fluid is still the best—it contains detergent to clean the windshield, and antifreeze to prevent it from freezing in the reservoir or on the windshield.

Season:
Because it rains most often in springtime in most climates, there may be a decrease in the prevalence of this stain then. Similarly, since water can be used in place of wiper fluid during warm weather, there may be fewer stains in summer.

Areas of Occurrence:
Windshield wiper fluid is peculiar in that it hardly ever stains when it is in use, because its use occurs outside the vehicle. Its activation occurs inside—where you are protected by the windshield being cleaned—so a stain will most likely occur as you fill the reservoir and the fluid splashes. Filling up the windshield wiper fluid in your car

exposes gloves, scarves, and the sleeves and fronts of jackets and sweaters to the possibility of a stain.

REMOVAL:

1. Rinse back of stain well with cold water or club soda.

2. If the stain remains, rub with dishwashing liquid or liquid enzyme detergent. Let stand several minutes. (Do not use bar or natural soap of any kind on the fabric or the stain will set.)

3. Rinse well with cold water.

4. Launder according to garment label.

5. If the stain remains, rub it with liquid enzyme detergent, then soak and agitate in cold water for 30 minutes or until the stain is removed.

6. Rinse well.

7. Apply laundry presoak (spot stain remover) and let stand several minutes.

8. Launder according to garment label.

Bodily Functions

88. **BLOOD**

General
Description:

The fluid that circulates in the principal vascular system of human beings and other vertebrates, in humans consisting of plasma in which the red blood cells, white blood cells, and platelets are suspended. Blood is one of the most precious substances in the world; produced by the body, it enables us to stay alive. In the second it takes to turn the page of this book, you will lose about three million red blood cells. During that same period, your bone marrow will have produced the same number of new ones. In an extreme emergency, the liquid inside young coconuts can be used as a substitute for blood plasma— a fact discovered by doctors in Fiji during World War II.

Season:

Unfortunately, bloodstains are not limited by season. Humans run the risk of stains from this precious fluid at every turn, in cases of accidental scrapes, cuts, and scratches. There are a few times of year when blood-stains may be more prevalent—for instance, during hunting seasons, when the blood that does the staining belongs to an animal that falls prey to the hunter's wiles. Women of childbearing age know to guard against bloodstains for about one week each month. And some, like doctors, nurses, workers in meat-pack-ing plants, and people who think they're vampires, must be vigilant every day of the year.

Areas of
Occurrence:

Blood can reach any area of any garment, and sometimes even furniture or carpeting. Some especially vulnerable places include the knees and elbows of children's clothes, as scrapes are common in these areas; the ankle area of socks, where blisters often occur; undergarments; sheets; the seats of chairs; and white skirts or pants (as they seem to attract the stuff).

Time of
Occurrence:

Bloodstains can happen at any time of the day or night, but stains resulting from malicious acts are more likely at night, in dark alleys and places better left unvisited. Benign stains caused by cuts and scrapes, as well as from menstruation, occur year-round.

Variations of
Significance:

Raw meat

REMOVAL: *On fabric:*

1. Rinse the stain immediately and thoroughly with cold saltwater. Do not use hot water or the stain will set. For dried stains, soak in cold saltwater up to 30 minutes or until the stain is loosened.

2. If the stain remains, soak in a mixture of liquid enzyme detergent and cold water for up to 30 minutes.

3. Rinse well.

4. If the stain remains, moisten cornstarch, baking soda, or unseasoned meat tenderizer and rub it into the stain to absorb some of the blood. Let the fabric dry in direct sunlight to further bleach the stain.

5. Brush the powder off once the garment is fully dry.

6. Rinse well with cold water.

7. Apply laundry presoak (spot stain remover) to any remaining stain and let stand several minutes.

8. Launder with liquid enzyme detergent.

On carpet:

1. Use a dull knife or spoon to remove as much as possible.

2. Blot remaining liquid with an absorbent cloth.

3. Sponge the stain with a sudsy mixture of liquid enzyme detergent and cold water, then sponge with cold, clean water. Repeat until you have removed as much stain as possible.

4. If the stain remains, sponge with a mild bleach, such as lemon juice or hydrogen peroxide (do not saturate carpet) then sponge with cold clear water. Repeat as needed.

5. If the stain remains, treat with a carpet spotter according to manufacturer's directions.

89.   **EXCREMENT**

General Description:

A waste matter discharged from the body, especially feces. There's no getting around the fact that most people turn up their noses at excrement. Even though it comes from the body and is natural, it's just not terribly pleasant stuff. Many people are used to dodging doggie-do on the sidewalks, but that's a sight that's less and less common these days due to more stringent laws. Before the enactment of the 1978 law that made it mandatory for dog owners in New York City to clean up after their pets, approximately 40 million pounds of dog excrement were deposited on the streets of that city each year.

Season:

Since both people and animals must empty their bowels regularly, even daily, excrement stains can occur any time of year.

Areas of Occurrence:

During an accident, a person can embarrassingly stain his or her own undergarments, trousers, or bed linens.

When changing a baby or cleaning out the litter box, those who neglect to roll up his or her sleeves beforehand may fall victim to this particularly nasty stain. The same goes for cleaning up after Rover in the park. In some instances, the act of cleaning up a pet's or child's excrement might result in stains on the fronts of jackets or sweaters, but these will hopefully be rare.

Time of Occurrence: Since adults do not soil themselves as a matter of course, this sort of stain knows no particular time. Early morning or late night are the most common hours for incurring a stain while cleaning up after a pet or changing a baby, since grogginess may undermine vigilance during these times.

REMOVAL:

1. Use a dull knife or spoon to remove as much as possible.

 2. For fresh stains, soak and agitate the fabric thoroughly in cold water. For dried stains, soak fabric in a soapy mixture of cold water and liquid enzyme detergent for 30 minutes or until the stain is loosened. Rinse well.

3. If the stain remains, rub a liquid enzyme detergent into the stain and let stand several minutes.

 4. Launder according to garment label.

5. If the stain remains, soak in an enzyme detergent mixture and cold water mixture up to 30 minutes.

 6. Rinse well.

 7. Apply a laundry presoak (spot stain remover) and launder again. On white fabrics, especially baby clothes, bleach any remaining stain by blotting with lemon juice and setting to dry in the sun.

90. **RING AROUND THE COLLAR**

General Description:

A build-up of sweat and dirt on the part of a shirt, coat, dress, blouse, or jacket that encompasses the neckline of the garment, often designed to fold or roll over. This pesky laundry problem gets worse the longer it sits. When ring around the collar is noticed, it should be taken care of as soon as possible. This stain came into the spotlight in the 1980s; Wisk detergent had a successful advertising campaign at that time, promising to eradicate ring around the collar when applied directly to shirts and blouses before laundering.

Season:

Summer is a time when this stain is probably more common, as sweat is the main ingredient of ring around the collar. However, since collared, button-down dress shirts are worn throughout the year with suits and jackets, this stain will appear throughout the year.

Areas of
Occurrence:
As the name indicates, this stain is found only on the collars and necklines of garments.

Time of
Occurrence:
This stain is caused by buildup, so the time of incurring the stain is largely indeterminate. You are likely to notice the stain in the evening, after five o'clock, when changing out of office garb and into loungewear.

REMOVAL:

1. Scrub collar with liquid laundry detergent. Let stand several minutes.

2. Launder in the hottest water safe for the fabric.

3. If the stain remains, let air dry and repeat steps 1 and 2. For particularly stubborn stains, apply a laundry presoak (spot stain remover) and launder again.

---

91. **SEMEN**

General
Description:
The viscid, whitish fluid produced in the male reproductive organs, containing spermatozoa. On average, a man ejaculates fourteen gallons of semen in his lifetime, and reproduces only an average of about 1.2 children, in the United States. This amounts to quite a bit of semen that does not reach its destination, which in turn leads to quite a few stained sheets.

Season: Semen knows no season—the human male is always ready to reproduce. Risk of staining increases, however, around the fourteenth of February each year, as well as during the time "spring fever," which is epidemic, strikes.

Areas of Occurrence: Sheets, pants, underwear, and towels are common places to find this stain, but it is possible for semen to wind up on any piece of clothing after being swept up in the moment. Semen has been discovered as far from the mark as the floor, a T-shirt, pajama top, dress, the pillowcase, even a curtain, following extreme carelessness.

Time of Occurrence: This stain may occur at any time, but early morning and late night are standard. Stains are usually found in the morning, either because they've just been created, or because daylight exposes evidence from last night's activities.

REMOVAL:

1. **Hold fabric stain-side down under cold running water to force water through fabric.**

2. **Soak and agitate the fabric in cold water until loosened.**

3. **If the stain remains, rub liquid laundry detergent into the stain and let stand several minutes.**

4. **Launder according to garment label.**

92. **SWEAT**

General
Description:

The moisture exuded from the body during strenuous activity; perspiration. This is one stain that every human being encounters at least once in his or her lifetime. It is truly universal, and it is one of the most irritating stains worldwide. While not typically subject to stains from this fluid, other animals most certainly sweat. Though the average person sweats two and a half quarts every day, it is nothing when compared with the camel. These humped creatures lose up to 30 percent of their body weight in perspiration and still continue crossing the desert. A human would die of heatstroke after losing just 12 percent of his or her body weight.

Season:

Since the body perspires when it needs to cool down, sweat stains aren't generally limited to a particular time of year, though summer's heat may increase the occurrence of these stains. During the winter cold-and-flu season, with its fevers and heavy blankets, sweat stains may also spike.

Areas of
Occurrence:

Undoubtedly the most common spot for a sweat stain is the armpit areas of T-shirts, turtlenecks, blouses, and dresses. This stain is the worst because the area is subject to much repeat staining, making the yellowing of the fabric there especially nasty. All pieces of workout clothing are subject to this stain, particularly T-shirts, tank tops, and sports bras. In the summer, bed linens are susceptible to this stain, especially in locales requiring air-conditioning.

REMOVAL:

1. Sponge the stain with ammonia or white vinegar. For heavy stains, rub with liquid laundry detergent and soak, occasionally rubbing stain between thumbs, until loosened.

2. Rinse well.

3. Repeat steps 1 and 2 until no more stain can be removed.

4. If the stain remains, apply laundry presoak (spot stain remover) and let stand several minutes.

5. Launder with a bleach that is safe for the fabric.

---

93. **URINE**

General Description:

The liquid-to-semisolid waste matter excreted by the kidneys, in humans being a yellowish, slightly acid, watery fluid. Urine stains are usually yellow and are always embarrassing. Whether the stain is made by an excited dog, a crying baby, or oneself when in a drunken stupor, it should be removed as soon as it occurs.

Season: Urine stains can happen at any time, especially to young children and, subsequently, their parents. There are particular times when adults might experience incontinence, namely during summer when the blockbuster comedic movies debut, and the extreme cold of winter, when blasts of air can be shocking in more than one way. Folks prone to drinking large amounts of alcohol might also find they experience troubling urine stains throughout the year.

Areas of Occurrence: 	One's own urine stains are generally limited to a few areas, including underwear and the crotch areas of pants. Sheets are a likely target for small children, while babies may produce urine stains on their parents' waists, on furniture, and sometimes even on ceilings if their diapers are off. For babies, there is no escaping this stain—all garments are at risk.
Time of Occurrence:	Urine stainings are most likely after 9 P.M., when the children are in bed, or much later, around 2 A.M., after the local pub closes.

REMOVAL: *For fresh stains on fabric:*

1. **Rinse well with cold water.**

2. **If the stain remains, mix a solution of 1 tablespoon ammonia in ½ cup warm water. Sponge the mixture over the stain and rinse well.**

3. If the stain remains, apply a laundry presoak (spot stain remover) and let stand several minutes.

 4. Launder according to garment label.

 5. If the stain remains, dilute hydrogen peroxide with water at a ratio of 1 to 4. Sponge the dilution on the stain, then rinse well with warm water. Repeat as needed.

For dried stains on fabric:

 1. Soak and agitate stain in cold water up to 1 hour.

2. Rub a liquid enzyme detergent into stain. Let stand several minutes. For persistent stains, rub with detergent, then soak in cold water for 30 minutes to 1 hour.

 3. Launder according to garment label.

 4. If the stain remains, launder with a bleach that is safe for the fabric. Test first for colorfastness.

On carpet:

1. Blot as much stain as possible with an absorbent cloth.

2. Sponge the stain with a sudsy mixture of cold water and liquid enzyme detergent. Scrub the stain with an old toothbrush and let stand 15 to 20 minutes.

3. Sponge with a clean, damp cloth, then blot with a dry cloth.

4. Repeat steps 2 and 3 until no more stain can be removed.

5. Allow carpet to dry thoroughly. Direct a fan onto the stain, if possible.

6. If an odor remains, repeat steps 2 through 5.

7. Once odor is eliminated, apply a carpet spotter according to manufacturer's directions.

8. If the stain lightens the carpet, sponge with a mild solution of 1 teaspoon ammonia to 1 cup water to restore the color. Test first for colorfastness.

9. Sponge with a clean, damp cloth, then blot with a dry cloth.

94. **VOMIT**

General
Description:

The substance that is forced from the stomach during regurgitation or throwing up, comprised of whatever was recently ingested by the sufferer along with stomach acids and juices. This stain is unique in that it can vary significantly according to its makeup, which changes depending on what the vomiter has lately consumed. Names for vomiting also vary—across cultures and across nations. In Denmark it's "talking into the big phone," and in Great Britain it's "playing the porcelain euphonium." Perhaps no country has more euphemisms for vomiting than the United States—among them are "praying to the porcelain god," "laughing at the carpet," "Technicolor yawn," "Ralphing," "booting," "hurling," and the classic "barfing."

Season:

This stain knows no season, as a night of too much drinking or a bite of rotten food that causes vomiting may take place any time of year. You might notice an increase in the occurrence of this stain during flu season, when many sufferers are unable to keep anything in their stomachs.

Areas of
Occurrence:

Pant legs and the fronts of blouses, sweaters, and jackets are particularly susceptible to this stain, especially when too much alcohol causes an upset stomach. Sickness from liquor will also render carpets and the walls of bathrooms vulnerable, as well as the cuffs of pants, and shoes and socks. When food poisoning or the flu is what's making you sick, nightgowns, pajamas, and robes are particularly at risk. Either situation can cause stains on sheets, blankets, and pillowcases, so you should be careful when resting. The school year is a sickness-prone time for some college students who go to frat parties or formal dances, so fancy dresses and tuxedos, as well as any party clothes, are at risk then.

Time of
Occurrence:
Throwing up is an activity not limited to a certain time of day, unfortunately. Depending on the vomiter's level of incoherence—whether alcohol- or virus-induced—the resulting vomit stain may be more likely occur during the wee hours of the night.

REMOVAL: *On fabric:*

1. Use a dull knife or spoon to remove as much as possible.

2. Flush the back of the stain well with cold water.

3. Dilute ammonia with warm water at a ratio of 1 to 4. Sponge the mixture into the stain.

4. Rinse well.

5. If the stain remains, soak in a sudsy mixture of liquid enzyme detergent and warm water until the stain is removed or up to 1 hour.

6. If the stain remains, apply laundry presoak (spot stain remover).

7. Launder according to garment label.

On carpet:

1. Use a dull knife or spoon to remove as much as possible.

2. Pour club soda on stain. Let stand several seconds.

3. Blot with an absorbent cloth. Replace cloth as it becomes saturated.

4. Repeat steps 2 and 3 as needed.

5. If the stain remains, treat with a carpet spotter according to manufacturer's directions.

Bathroom and Beauty Products

95. **BABY OIL**

General
Description:

Nontoxic oil, usually mineral oil, which maintains its clear color regardless of temperature and often has a pleasant scent. Baby oil is a favorite of parents everywhere for its use as a skin-softening agent for babies and adults alike. It is appreciated by others, too, including bodybuilders, admirers of the sun, and makeup artists who want their subjects to have the appearance of a sweaty glow.

Season:

Though birthings are constant, baby-oil stains increase during the sunny summer months, when devoted sun-worshippers slather themselves with the stuff while striving for the perfect tan.

Areas of
Occurrence:

The area affected by a baby-oil stain depends on how you employ the oil. When used to keep a baby's skin supple, it might stain baby's clothes or blankets. When used to enhance the effects of the sun's rays, it might stain bathing suits, towels, shorts, or sundresses. And when used by a bodybuilder to draw attention to shining muscles, Speedos or string bikinis may bear the stain.

REMOVAL:

1. Use a dull knife or spoon to remove as much as possible.

2. Blot remaining liquid with an absorbent cloth.

3. Sprinkle salt, baking soda, cornstarch, or talcum powder on stain to absorb excess oil and let stand 10 to 15 minutes, then brush off.

4. Rub colorless dishwashing liquid into stain. Let stand 1 to 2 minutes.

5. Soak in a sudsy mixture of hot water and dishwashing liquid for up to 30 minutes.

6. Rinse the back of the stain well with hot water.

7. Use a dull knife or spoon again to remove any loosened oil from the fabric.

8. If the stain remains, make a paste of baking soda and water at a ratio of approximately 3 to 1, spread on stain and let dry, then brush off.

9. Apply laundry presoak (spot stain remover) and let stand several minutes to penetrate fabric.

10. Launder in the hottest water safe for the fabric. For extra-heavy stains, replace half the amount of detergent with baking soda.

96. **BLUSH OR ROUGE**

General
Description:

Any of various red-tinted cosmetics used for coloring the cheeks. Since most people try to hide their embarrassment and are further embarrassed when caught in a scarlet blush, it seems odd that there is a desire to imitate this reddening. Odd or no, people have been artificially reddening their cheeks for centuries. In the eighteenth century, both women and men used rouge at great risk. The beauty product was made of a sulfur and mercury compound, and caused inflamed gums and tooth loss.

Season:

This is one of the few cosmetics that is typically seasonal, because its application may be discontinued during summer, when the sun lends a natural pink glow to the cheeks. Winter may therefore be a more likely time to find this stain. Those involved with theater, however, will probably incur this stain year-round, as stage lights wash out even the pinkest faces.

Areas of
Occurrence:

Blush and rouge stains can appear almost anywhere, depending upon whether it is your own blush or another party's that is responsible for the staining. Your own blush is likely to show itself on the collar or front of your blouse or jacket, or on your coat or scarf, as the weather becomes colder. Another's blush could appear on the front of a dress shirt, or on a necktie. During opening night at the theater or anytime during the run of a production, rouge can find its way onto any article of an actor's clothing, due to quick changes in the wings.

Time of
Occurrence:

When the blush in question is your own, it will usually appear as a stain during application—in the morning before work or in the evening before a date. If another person's blush is to blame for the stain, it was most likely achieved during a romantic encounter—usually in the evening.

REMOVAL:

1. Use a dull knife or spoon to remove as much as possible.

2. Dampen stain and rub with bar soap, dishwashing liquid, or liquid laundry detergent. Rub the stain between thumbs.

3. Rinse well.

4. Repeat steps 2 and 3 until no more stain can be removed.

5. If the stain remains, especially if makeup is oily, soak in a sudsy mixture of water and detergent for 10 to 15 minutes.

6. Rinse well.

7. If the stain remains, treat with a laundry presoak (spot stain remover).

8. Launder according to garment label.

97. DEODORANTS OR ANTIPERSPIRANTS

General Description:

Deodorant: *A substance used to inhibit or mask perspiration or other bodily odors.* Antiperspirant: *An astringent preparation for reducing perspiration, usually containing aluminum or zirconium and used to prevent body odor.* The skin of the armpits can harbor up to 516,000 bacteria per square inch, while drier areas, such as the forearm, have only about 13,000 bacteria per square inch. For this reason, in many cultures adults apply deodorants and antiperspirants to their armpits to prevent excessive sweat and odor. These substances are available in many forms, including roll-on liquids, sprays, gels, solids, powders, and in some cases, even natural crystals. In a pinch, chamomile tea or rosemary can be used as effective deodorants. Wet the tea bag or the herb, and rub it on the offending areas. If possible, leave in place for a few minutes.

Season:

Perspiration, and thus stains from deodorants and antiperspirants, occurs all year long, but it is much more prevalent during the balmy summer months, when the use of deodorant is demanded.

Areas of
Occurrence:

Stains from deodorants and antiperspirants will be
found not only in the armpit areas of clothes, but also
on the sides and waist areas of pull-over shirts or dresses.
In the summer there is also a chance that such stains
will mysteriously materialize on other areas of clothing,
for instance the backs or shoulders of T-shirts and dresses,
especially after cuddling with a freshly showered and
groomed loved one.

Time of
Occurrence:

Antiperspirant and deodorant stains are two of the most
opportunistic—they tend to present themselves at the
least advantageous times, such as just before work, in
the moments leading up to a blind date, and other
times when grooming is rushed and of the utmost
importance.

REMOVAL: *For fresh stains on fabric:*

1. Mix a laundry presoak (spot stain remover) with
   lukewarm water and sponge on the dry fabric
   stain. Let stand several minutes.

2. Rinse well.

3. Repeat steps 1 and 2 until no more stain can be
   removed.

4. If the stain damages color, restore it by sponging
   the damaged area with ammonia. If treating wool

or silk for a stain, dilute ammonia with an equal amount of water.

5. Rinse well.

 6. Launder in the hottest water safe for the fabric.

For dried stains on fabric:

1. Mix a laundry presoak (spot stain remover) and lukewarm water. Place stain face-down on an absorbent cloth and sponge the back of it with the mixture. Let stand several minutes.

2. Rinse well. Repeat until no more stain can be removed.

3. Rub liquid enzyme detergent into the stain.

4. Launder in the hottest water safe for the fabric.

5. If fabric has discolored, restore by blotting with white vinegar.

6. Rinse well.

98. **EYELINER OR EYE SHADOW**

General
Description:

Eyeliner: *A cosmetic applied in a thin line along the eye lids, usually next to the lashes, to accentuate the eyes.* Eye shadow: *A cosmetic coloring material, usually a powder or cream, applied to the eyelids.* Eye makeup has gone through many changes in its long history. Iridescent beetle shells were the source of the earliest eye glitter used, devised by the ancient Egyptians. Nowadays, synthetic materials are used to make both eyeliner and shadow, and the styles are endless. From cat-eye tails made with liner in the 1960s to blue shadow up to the brows in the 1980s to having liner permanently tattooed on the lids in the twenty-first century, eye-enhancement has certainly changed over the years.

Season:

Eye makeup knows no season, though the colors worn during summer may differ from those worn in winter. Beauty-conscious women and transvestites alike wouldn't be caught dead leaving home without it.

Areas of
Occurrence:

Perhaps the most common—and certainly the most irritating—occurrence of this stain happens not when applying either substance, but when shadow or liner opens or breaks in a handbag or suitcase. This results in stains not only on the lining of the bag, but on any items in close proximity to the cosmetic. Of course, sloppiness with shadow or liner may result in stains to sleeves or fronts of blouses or dresses as well.

| Time of Occurrence: | Anytime makeup needs a touch-up is a time for this stain to occur, but more likely times are the morning before work or the evening before a date, when you are perfecting the beauty ritual. |

REMOVAL:

1. Use a dull knife or spoon to remove as much as possible.

 2. Dampen stain and rub with bar soap, dishwashing liquid, or liquid laundry detergent. Rub the stain between thumbs.

 3. Rinse well.

4. Repeat steps 2 and 3 until no more stain can be removed.

5. If the stain remains, especially if makeup is oily, soak in a sudsy mixture of water and detergent for 10 to 15 minutes.

 6. Rinse well.

 7. If the stain remains, treat with a laundry presoak (spot stain remover).

 8. Launder according to garment label.

99. **FOUNDATION**

General
Description:

A cosmetic, usually in cream or liquid form, that is used as a base for facial makeup. Worn by many women and even a few men, foundation smoothes the tone and texture of the skin. It comes in a variety of forms, including powder, liquid, pan, and stick, with the latter three being the most likely to cause staining. Most people wear foundation only on their faces, though some, especially those involved in the theater, movies, or the television industry, wear it on their necks and chests as well.

Season:

Foundation stains are seen more often in winter, when tans have faded and people are inclined to use more makeup to deepen the color of their skin. However, if foundation is worn in summer, the heat and perspiration may cause it to run, making a stain very likely.

Areas of
Occurrence:

Foundation stains are found on the collars of shirts and dresses, but may also be found on pants, skirts, carpets, and towels, if dropped or spilled. A foundation stain is not limited to women's attire—it might present itself on men's clothes, on collars, shoulders, and chest areas of shirts or jackets, and even in the crotch or lap area of pants. Bed linens are another high-risk area, especially when you are in too big a hurry to wash your face before going to bed.

Time of
Occurrence:

Stains from foundation may occur in the hours before or during a night on the town, as foundation is sometimes applied more heavily later in the day. Some choose to wear foundation at work, so another prime time for stains is in the early morning.

Removal:

1. Use a dull knife or spoon to remove as much as possible.

2. Dampen stain and rub with bar soap, dishwashing liquid, or liquid laundry detergent. Rub the stain between thumbs.

3. Rinse well.

4. Repeat steps 2 and 3 until no more stain can be removed.

5. If the stain remains, especially if makeup is oily, soak in a sudsy mixture of water and detergent for 10 to 15 minutes.

6. Rinse well.

7. If the stain remains, treat with a laundry presoak (spot stain remover).

8. Launder according to garment label.

100. **LIP BALM**

General
Description:
An oil-based substance used to moisturize the lips to keep them from becoming chapped or dry. Lips are primarily mucous membrane, which has fewer glands than ordinary skin. The outer layer is very thin or even nonexistent in most people. Lips also have no melanin, the natural pigment in skin that helps block the sun's harmful ultraviolet rays. Because of these properties, lips tend to dry out very quickly—weather and other factors often help speed up this process—which leaves many people with the annoyance of chapped lips. Although "lip balm addiction" has become a popular buzz-word of late, industry experts assert that there is no addictive ingredient in lip balm. No resistance builds up and no withdrawal symptoms occur if you choose to stop using lip balm.

Season:

Due to the increase in painful chapping of lips during the cold dry months of the year, lip balm stains are twice as likely to occur during winter. Anytime you are sick with a cold or flu is a time this stain might appear, also due to increased chapping.

Areas of
Occurrence:

Lip balm is invariably put away without its cap, or with its cap loosely applied, which ensures a lip balm stain on the insides of jacket and trouser pockets, as well as the linings of purses and backpacks. Individuals confined to bed with a cold may cause these stains on pillowcases or sheets, too, especially if a fever is involved.

Time of
Occurrence:

Since lip balm is applied and reapplied throughout the day, there is rarely immunity to this stain, no matter what time of day.

REMOVAL:

1. Use a dull knife or spoon to remove as much as possible.

2. Dampen stain and rub with bar soap, dishwashing liquid, or liquid laundry detergent. Rub the stain between thumbs.

3. Rinse well.

4. Repeat steps 2 and 3 until no more stain can be removed.

5. If the stain remains, especially if makeup is oily, soak in a sudsy mixture of water and detergent for 10 to 15 minutes.

6. Rinse well.

7. If the stain remains, treat with a laundry presoak (spot stain remover).

8. Launder according to garment label.

101. **LIPSTICK**

General
Description:

A waxy cosmetic in stick form used to color the lips.
Thought to be a beauty enhancer, lipstick is worn by
many women around the world. Made from wax, oil,
pearl essence (the silvery substance in the skin of herring
and other fishes), dyes, and fragrances, lipstick has
evolved as an essential part of modern war paint.

Season:

This substance knows no season; beauty-conscious
women and cross-dressers alike are never seen in public
without it. Intense colors with tan hues are more often
used in colder months, while paler, pastel shades are
worn in spring and summer.

Areas of
Occurrence:

Lipstick stains can appear almost anywhere. Your own
lipstick is likely to show itself on the sleeves of your
blouse or jacket, especially if no napkins are handy at
dinner. The lipstick from another may appear on your
collar, front of a dress shirt, or on a necktie. Sometimes
a lipstick tube will get into the laundry, and once in the
dryer, it melts and stains all garments with which it
comes in contact.

Variations of
Significance:

Lip balm; lip gloss; lip liner; lipstick sealers

REMOVAL:

1. **Use a dull knife or spoon to remove as much
    as possible.**

2. Dampen stain and rub with bar soap, dishwashing liquid, or liquid laundry detergent. Rub the stain between thumbs.

3. Rinse well.

4. Repeat steps 2 and 3 until no more stain can be removed.

5. If the stain remains, especially if makeup is oily, soak in a sudsy mixture of water and detergent for 10 to 15 minutes.

6. Rinse well.

7. If the stain remains, treat with a laundry presoak (spot stain remover).

8. Launder according to garment label.

102. **LOTION, HAND, BODY, OR SUNTAN**

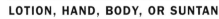

General Description: *A liquid, usually an aqueous but sometimes alcoholic preparation, containing insoluble material in the form of a suspension or emulsion, intended for external application, especially on the face or hands, and containing agents for soothing or softening the skin.* As Earth's atmosphere continues to change, lotion may be one of our best protectors against the sun's damaging rays.

Season: Lotion stains are widespread in winter, when an over-
whelming number of people are battling dry skin. This
is not to say that a stain is not possible at other times
of year—suntan lotion certainly takes its toll in stains
during the summer. Professionals who require frequent
hand-washing and water use, like nurses, doctors,
homemakers, and restaurant workers (especially in
the kitchen), will suffer lotion stains year-round.

Areas of Lotion stains appear everywhere as lotion can be—and
Occurrence: is—used on all parts of the body.

Variations of Tissues coated with lotion
Significance:

REMOVAL: *On fabric:*

1. Use a dull knife or spoon to remove as much as
    possible.

2. Blot remaining liquid with an absorbent cloth.

 3. Sprinkle salt, baking soda, cornstarch, or talcum
    powder on stain to absorb excess oil and let stand
    10 to 15 minutes, then brush off.

4. Rub colorless dishwashing liquid into stain. Let

stand 1 to 2 minutes.

5. Soak in a sudsy mixture of hot water and dish-washing detergent for up to 30 minutes.

 6. Rinse the back of the stain well with hot water.

7. Use a dull knife or spoon again to remove any loosened lotion from the fabric.

8. If the stain remains, make a paste of baking soda and water at a ratio of approximately 3 to 1, spread on stain and let dry, then brush off.

 9. Apply laundry presoak (spot stain remover) and let stand several minutes.

 10. Launder in the hottest water safe for the fabric. For extra-heavy stains, replace half the amount of detergent with baking soda.

11. If the stain remains, repeat steps 3 through 10.

On carpet:

1. Use a dull knife or spoon to remove as much as possible.

2. Blot remaining liquid with an absorbent cloth.

(For heavy or dark stains, it is best to call a professional cleaner.)

3. Sprinkle the stain with an absorbent powder, such as baking soda, cornstarch, cornmeal, or talcum powder. Let sit for 6 to 12 hours, then vacuum—do not brush the powder.

or

Spray with shaving cream and work into the carpet with an old toothbrush. Wipe with a damp cloth, then sponge with cold water.

or

Dampen with club soda and blot. Repeat as needed.

4. If the stain remains, apply dry-cleaning fluid (be careful not to wet the carpet backing with it) then sponge the stain with a damp cloth.

or

Treat with a carpet spotter according to manufacturer's directions.

---

103.   **MASCARA**

General
Description:

A cosmetic applied to the eyelashes to make them appear darker, longer, or fuller. Before mascara, fake eyelashes applied to eyelids with adhesive were a popular way to accentuate the eyes. Though they have long gone the way of 8-track players and the abacus, fake lashes are still an excellent alternative for those who fear the dreaded mascara stain. Basic brown or black mascara is still the choice for both women and cross-dressers who want to enhance their coquettish lash-batting abilities, though other colors are produced. Blue mascara enjoyed a brief popularity in the 1980s, and what would Halloween be without silver and gold?

Season:

Mascara is a year-round cosmetic, though the warmer months of summer may cause even the most expensive mascara to melt and run down the face and onto clothing while undressing.

Areas of
Occurrence:

The area underneath the eyes is without a doubt the most common staining ground for mascara; luckily, soap and water will generally remove this stain with no permanent damage. Watch for this stain on the sleeves of blouses and jackets, especially at the end ofa grueling day when the eyes simply had to be rubbed. The insides of camisoles, shirts, and dresses are vulnerable to this stain when they are hastily removed. Of course, sheets, pillows, and nightgowns are most at risk for mascara stainings if nighttime makeup removal is neglected.

Time of
Occurrence:

Late night hours are the most common for this stain, as exhaustion from a long day makes for careless rubbing of eyes and hasty removal of clothing. Early morning, before work, and evening, before a date, are also times when this stain may present itself, especially when you are short on preparation time.

REMOVAL:

1. Use a dull knife or spoon to remove as much as possible.

 2. Dampen stain and rub with bar soap, dishwashing liquid, or liquid laundry detergent. Rub the stain between thumbs.

3. Rinse well.

4. Repeat steps 2 and 3 until no more stain can be removed.

5. If the stain remains, especially if makeup is oily, soak in a sudsy mixture of water and detergent for 10 to 15 minutes.

 6. Rinse well.

 7. If the stain remains, treat with a laundry presoak (spot stain remover).

 8. Launder according to garment label.

104. **NAIL POLISH**

General
Description:

A polish of quick-drying lacquer, either clear or colored, used to paint the fingernails or toenails. Fingernail polish often contains four or five chemicals the U.S. Environmental Protection Agency calls potentially harmful. If a person bought fingernail polish in a 55-gallon drum, the empty drum could not be legally thrown into a landfill. It would have to be transported to the nearest state-regulated commercial hazardous-waste disposal facility.

Season:

Fashionable ladies (and even some gentlemen) apply nail polish at all times of year, especially when special occasions are on the agenda. However, during the warm months of spring and summer, when sandals are standard attire and pedicures are as regularly sought as manicures, the chances of acquiring this stain double.

Areas of
Occurrence:

Nail polish stains can be found anywhere if hands or feet are used too soon after application. These stains are standard on socks, gloves, pants, and stockings. Bedsheets and towels are possible stain sites as well.

Time of
Occurrence:

Nail polish stains can happen any time a person has time for pampering, be it early in the morning or while watching television sitcoms in the evening.

REMOVAL: *On fabric:*

1. Place the garment over an absorbent cloth and blot with an acetone nail polish remover. Straight acetone can also be used; it is stronger and may work faster than nail polish remover. For either method, test first for colorfastness. If color is affected, substitute white vinegar for the nail polish remover. Apply slowly and blot continuously. Replace the cloth as it becomes saturated.

2. Rinse well.

3. Repeat steps 1 and 2 until you have removed as much stain as possible.

4. Apply a laundry presoak (spot stain remover) and let stand several minutes.

5. Launder according to garment label.

6. Let fabric dry in the sun after each washing, for added bleaching. For white or colorfast materials, try blotting the stain with a solution of equal parts white vinegar or hydrogen peroxide and water, then setting fabric in sunlight. Keep stain moist with solution until the stain is removed. If all else fails, launder with a bleach that is safe for the fabric. Test first for colorfastness.

On carpet:

 1. Blot stain with an acetone nail polish remover. Straight acetone can also be used; it is stronger and may work faster than nail polish remover. For either method, test first for colorfastness. If color is affected, substitute white vinegar for the nail polish remover. Apply slowly and blot continuously. Blot well with clean water. Repeat until you have removed as much stain as possible.

2. If the stain remains, treat with a carpet spotter.

 3. Lighten the stain with a mild bleach, such as hydrogen peroxide, white vinegar, or lemon juice.

---

105. 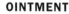 **OINTMENT**

General Description:
A soft, unctuous preparation, often medicated, for application to the skin. Ointments, also known as unguents, salves, unctions, and cerates, are applied to the skin to treat a variety of ailments, including bug bites, chafing, swollen tissue, and many other socially unmentionable dilemmas. Their use can bring relief from these afflictions but can also create embarrassing stains.

Season:
 Ointments have uses in all seasons—in summer, it might be for cuts, scrapes, rashes, or arthritic joints agi-

tated by athletic use; in winter, as a cure for dry or irritated skin, and as a medication to soothe coughs. Diaper rash, a seasonless ailment for young children, calls for treatment with ointmens and vigilance against their stains.

Areas of
Occurrence:

Ointment is not limited to a particular area of use and therefore its stains can be anywhere. Some commonly affected areas include pajama tops, athletic uniforms, undergarments, the elbow areas of sweatshirts and long-sleeved jerseys, the knee areas of pants and stockings, cloth diapers, and bed linens.

REMOVAL:

1. Use a dull knife or spoon to remove as much as possible.

2. Blot remaining stain with an absorbent cloth.

3. Sprinkle salt, baking soda, cornstarch, or talcum powder on stain to absorb excess ointment and let stand 10 to 15 minutes, then brush off.

4. Rub colorless dishwashing liquid into stain. Let stand 1 to 2 minutes.

5. Soak in a sudsy mixture of hot water and dishwashing liquid for up to 30 minutes.

6. Rinse the back of the stain well with hot water.

7. Use a dull knife or spoon to remove any loosened ointment from the fabric.

8. If the stain remains, make a paste of baking soda and water at a ratio of approximately 3 to 1, spread on stain and let dry, then brush off.

 9. Apply laundry presoak (spot stain remover) and let stand several minutes to penetrate fabric.

 10. Launder in the hottest water safe for the fabric. For extra-heavy stains, replace half the amount of detergent with baking soda.

On carpet:

1. Use a dull knife or spoon to remove as much as possible.

2. Blot remaining liquid with an absorbent cloth. (For heavy or dark stains, it is best to call a professional cleaner.)

  3. Sprinkle the stain with an absorbent powder, such as baking soda, cornstarch, cornmeal, or talcum powder. Let sit for 6 to 12 hours, then vacuum (do not brush) the powder.

 or

Spray with shaving cream and work into the carpet

with an old toothbrush. Wipe with a damp cloth, then sponge with cold water.

or

Dampen with club soda and blot. Repeat as needed.

4. If the stain remains, apply dry-cleaning fluid (be careful not to wet the carpet backing with it), then sponge the stain with a damp cloth.

or

Treat with a carpet spotter according to manufacturer's directions.

---

106. **PERFUME**

General Description:
A substance that diffuses or imparts an agreeable or attractive smell, especially a fluid containing fragrant natural oils extracted from flowers, woods, etc., or similar synthetic oils. The conquest of Alexander the Great in the fourth century B.C. first brought perfume to Greece, and since that time, it has been a vital ingredient in the mating rituals of humans. Many people believe that scent is extremely important in attracting the opposite sex, basing their belief on the known allure of both formulated perfumes as well as the body's natural perfumes, called pheromones, which are secreted periodically. Perfume has a long history of helping to woo; legend has it that when setting out to meet Marc Antony, Cleopatra sprinkled perfume on the sails of her barge.

Season:

Both men and women like to smell good regardless of season, making perfume a year-round stain. The heat of summer sometimes facilitates the transfer of perfume from skin to clothing, so this stain may be a bit more common at this time of year.

Areas of Occurrence:

Perfume most frequently stains the cuffs and collars or neck areas of button-down blouses, dresses, and suit jackets. However, those who use perfume adventurously might find stains in such out-of-the-way spots as behind the knees of trousers, or on lacy undergarments. Unfortunately, as scents are generally packaged in glass bottles, there is a high incidence of breakage when these bottles are transported in pocketbooks or luggage. When this occurs, the linings of bags as well as any clothing that may be in the vicinity are affected.

REMOVAL:

1. **Rinse back of stain well with cold water or club soda.**

2. **If the stain remains, rub with dishwashing liquid or liquid enzyme detergent. Let stand several minutes. Do not use bar or natural soap of any kind on the fabric or the stain will set.**

3. **Rinse well with cold water.**

4. **Launder according to garment label.**

5. If the stain remains, rub it with liquid enzyme detergent, then soak and agitate in cold water for 30 minutes, or until the stain is removed.

 6. Rinse well.

 7. Apply laundry presoak (spot stain remover) and let stand several minutes.

 8. Launder according to garment label.

---

107. 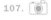 **TOOTHPASTE**

General Description:

A sticky, pasty substance used for cleaning the teeth; dentifrice. Toothpaste was invented by the Egyptians some five thousand years ago; it was a crude mixture of wine and pumice. These days, toothpaste is high tech. Not only does it come in an array of different containers—from flip-caps to complicated canisters—there are also different types that boast a variety of uses. Some include both paste and a gel, each serving a unique function; there are tartar control pastes, pastes that include mouthwash, whitening pastes, and pastes that are said to freshen the "whole mouth." Regardless of your preferred paste, a toothbrush, toothpaste, and dental floss are the necessary ingredients for overall dental hygiene.

Season:
Teeth need brushing year-round; there is no season for higher risk of obtaining a toothpaste stain.

Areas of
Occurrence:

The fronts of pajamas, nightgowns, and robes are particularly vulnerable to this stain, especially when you are groggy in the morning or just before bed. Toothpaste stains are often incurred on the fronts of blouses, jackets, and dresses, especially when you are hurried while getting ready to go out.

Time of
Occurrence:
Early in the morning before work and in the evening before going out for dinner or dancing are especially irksome times to experience this stain, because it often requires a costume change. Late at night before bed is another stain-prone time; the probability of a stain increases exponentially as the level of exhaustion increases.

REMOVAL:
1. **Use a dull knife or spoon to remove as much as possible.**

2. **Blot stain with a sudsy mixture of cold water and liquid enzyme detergent.**

3. **Rinse well. Repeat until no more stain can be removed.**

4. **Launder according to garment label.**

Office and School Products

108. 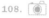 **ADHESIVES OR STICKERS**

General
Description:

Adhesive: *a substance that causes something to adhere, as glue or rubber cement.* Sticker: *an adhesive label.*
Adhesives and stickers have become omnipresent. From the "inspected by" sticker in the pocket of a new pair of pants to the price tag on a loaf of bread to the transparent tape sealing a wrapped present, adhesives and stickers are literally everywhere. In addition to the more commonly thought of uses, tape has been employed in some especially interesting places: Ornithologists often placed transparent tape over cracks in the soft shells of fertilized pigeon eggs, allowing the eggs to hatch. Tape has also been used as an anticorrosive shield on the Goodyear blimp. At one point transparent tape even repaired a torn original of the Declaration of Independence.

Season:

The season for stains from adhesives and stickers is boundless—you are just as likely to suffer a stain from a "HELLO, MY NAME IS" sticker on the lapel of a jacket in the winter months as from an errant piece of tape in the summer.

Areas of
Occurrence:

Stickers are maddening in their ability to stick undetected onto the back of a pant leg or to the hidden elbow of the arm on a shirt. Children, especially those with glasses, may find messages like KICK ME taped to the backs of their sweaters or uniforms hours after the sign first appeared, allowing plenty of time for the stain to take hold. Other areas where stains are found include the lapels of jackets and the upper chest region of sweaters, dresses, and blouses; anywhere a store might see fit to place a price sticker; the inside of a shirt, pants, or even a pocket, where inspectors place their stamp of approval; and the insides of garments worn over knees and elbows, where adhesive bandages have been used.

Variations of Significance:

"HELLO, MY NAME IS" stickers; adhesive bandages; duct tape; gold stars; price stickers; transparent tape

REMOVAL:

1. Rub an ice cube on the stain or place in the freezer. Use a dull knife or spoon to remove as much as possible.

2. Sponge the stain with eucalyptus oil, baby oil, or cooking oil until the stain is loosened. Use a dull knife or spoon to remove as much as possible.

3. Rinse well.

4. Repeat steps 2 and 3 until you've removed as much stain as possible.

5. Sponge the stain with a laundry presoak (spot stain remover).

6. Launder according to garment label.

7. If the stain remains, place it facedown on an absorbent cloth and apply dry-cleaning fluid to the back of the stain. Use the fluid according to manufacturer's directions. Let the stain dry.

  8. Rinse thoroughly.

  9. Launder according to garment label.

On glass or metal surfaces:

  1. If adhesive is water-soluble, sponge with warm sudsy water or cover with a warm, wet cloth and let stand several minutes. If adhesive is solvent-based, sponge with nail polish remover or acetone until softened. Test first in an inconspicuous area.

2. Once softened, use a dull knife or spoon to remove as much as possible.

3. Repeat steps 1 and 2 as needed.

109. **CARBON PAPER OR COPIER TONER**

General
Description:

Carbon paper: *A paper faced with a preparation of carbon or other material, used between two sheets of plain paper to copy on the lower sheet what is written or typed on the upper.* Copier toner: *A powder, either dry or dispersed in organic liquid, used in photocopiers and xerography to produce a final image.* Though carbon paper is rarely used today (artists still employ it), it has left its mark on future technology; the e-mail function "cc" indicates that a "carbon copy" of the electronic image will be sent. Copier toner, however, is still used in office buildings around the globe and causes no small amount of trouble. Due to its powdery consistency as well as the largely enigmatic nature of copy machines, toner is very likely to make a mess.

Season:

Toner must be replaced in copy machines every few months, depending on the volume of work the machine handles, so these stains appear throughout the year.

Areas of
Occurrence:

Stains incurred from carbon paper are most likely to be on the fingers and hands of the person using it; the most common way a stain will appear is when you rub the affected area on clothing. Pants, jackets, and dress shirts are also likely victims of this stain. Toner, however, is far wilier, and its stains often appear on shoes, socks, the bottoms of pant legs, carpeting, and any other fabric unlucky enough to be in the path of the toner cartridge.

Time of
Occurrence:

It is unlikely that stains from these products will be incurred at any time of day other than between the hours of 9 A.M. and 5 P.M., when offices are in full swing.

REMOVAL:

1. Shake off as much loose powder as possible. Hold the garment over the sink and tap the back of the stain lightly with an old toothbrush to help remove powder.

2. Brush the stain carefully with the toothbrush. Do not touch the stain with your hand; the oil on your skin will spread the stain.

3. Sponge the stain liberally with soapy water until you have removed as much as possible.

4. If the stain remains, apply a laundry presoak (spot stain remover) and let stand several minutes.

5. Launder in the hottest water safe for the fabric.

---

110. **CHALK**

General
Description:

A soft, compact calcite, derived chiefly from tiny plankton fossils. Commonly used by teachers as a tool for communicating with students, chalk can be found in classrooms and in teachers' pockets around the world. Chalk has served a number of purposes in addition to teachers' tool—in Victorian England, milk contained chalk as an additive for purely aesthetic reasons.

Season:

This stain appears throughout the school year. It is much more rare during summer months, but those attending summer school and children fond of drawing on sidewalks are susceptible to this stain even in summer.

Areas of
Occurrence:

For educators, their seats of pants and skirts and their sweaters are common areas for this stain. However, chalk and its dust are far-reaching due to their powdery consistency, and they can therefore be found on the sleeves of jackets as well as shoes and backpacks. For students, chalk dust may be wiped almost anywhere, from socks to mittens. Additionally, the student with a naughty streak might find herself covered from head to foot in the stuff after an eraser-banging chastisement.

Time of
Occurrence:

Chalk stains almost always occur during the day, between the hours of 9 a.m. and 3 p.m., except when they occur during the aforementioned after-school punishment. Occasionally these stains may crop up on the weekends, when children take to the streets for hopscotch. You might even incur this stain in the evening, during a night class. Gymnasts, baseball pitchers, artists, and policemen often obtain this stain during their work hours.

Variations of
Significance:

Chewable antacids

REMOVAL:

1. Shake garment outdoors or vacuum to remove as much loose chalk as possible.

2. Place fabric stain-down over an absorbent cloth and blot the back of the stain with rubbing alcohol. Replace cloth as it becomes saturated.

  3. Rinse well.

4. Repeat steps 2 and 3 until you have removed as much chalk as possible.

5. Rub liquid detergent into the stain and let stand several minutes.

  6. Launder according to garment label.

---

111.   **CORRECTION FLUID**

General Description:

An opaque, quick-drying fluid used to obliterate handwritten or typewritten matter. Bette Nesmith, the mother of former Monkee Mike Nesmith, invented correction fluid. She later named the product Liquid Paper and, in 1979, sold the rights to the Gillette Company for $47.5 million. This product has since become a staple in desk drawers everywhere, be it in the home or in the office. Editors, secretaries, students, accountants, and many government workers can't imagine working without it.

Season:

Correction fluid creates stains throughout the year, but such stains may be particularly widespread during the hectic days of tax season.

Areas of Occurrence:

Stains from this helpful fluid are prevalent on the arms of collared shirts and on dresses, and any other garment suitable for office attire. Other affected areas may include tabletops, carpeting, upholstered furniture, and the cloth walls of an office cubicle.

Time of Occurrence:

Students and taxpayers prone to procrastination might encounter this stain during late-night or very early morning hours, but it is most commonly acquired from 9 A.M. to 5 P.M.

Variations of Significance:

Correction tape

REMOVAL:

1. Spray both sides of fabric with WD-40™ to loosen the stain. Let stand until the stain is loosened (dab with fingers to see if any comes off).

2. Rinse well.

3. Lay stain facedown on absorbent cloth. Saturate back of stain with nail polish remover. Turn garment over and sponge surface of stain with nail polish remover. You can also substitute acetone for nail polish remover for a stronger approach; use

according to manufacturer's directions.

4. Rinse well.

5. Repeat steps 3 and 4 until you have removed as much stain as possible.

 6. Apply a laundry presoak (spot stain remover) and let stand several minutes.

7. Launder according to garment label.

---

112. **CRAYON**

General Description: *A pointed stick made of colored chalk or wax, used for drawing or coloring.* Crayons are practically synonymous with the brand-name Crayola, which is a combination of the French word *craie*, "chalk" and *ola*, from "oleaginous," meaning oily. Emerson Moser, who was Crayola's senior crayon maker for 37 years, revealed upon his retirement that he was colorblind. He molded more than 1.4 billion crayons during his career.

Season: Children and artists alike use crayons for their art projects throughout the year; however, parents generally find crayon stains on their children's clothing during the school year. Younger children are probably the most likely to experience the most crayon stains over the course of the year.

Areas of
Occurrence:

Depending upon the user's level of creativity, crayons may stain sleeves of T-shirts, sweaters, and jackets, to pant legs and shoes. An art teacher might employ smocks in his or her classroom, so stains also appear on the fronts and sleeves of these coverings. Walls and flooring are also common places to find crayon stains, especially in households containing particularly boisterous tots.

Time of
Occurrence:

The hours between 9 A.M. and 3 P.M. are the most likely times to obtain this stain, though these stains aren't limited to the school day. Coloring is a favorite pastime of children all over the world, and parents are often grateful for the quiet moments in the evening when youngsters busy themselves with books and crayons. The wee hours of the night are a time when crayon stains rarely occur, though artists who use crayons might find the muse striking late into the night.

REMOVAL:

1. **Place stained item on absorbent paper towels. Spray each side with WD-40™, letting stand several minutes after each application.**

2. **Rinse well.**

3. **Rub dishwashing liquid into the stain with a damp cloth. Replace the cloth as it becomes saturated with crayon. Repeat until no more crayon is removed.**

4. Rinse well.

 5. Apply a laundry presoak (spot stain remover) and let stand several minutes.

 6. Launder in the hottest water safe for the fabric.

7. If the stain remains, let dry in sunlight and repeat steps 1 through 6.

On a hard surface, such as wood, tile, or paneling:

1. Spray stain with WD-40™ to loosen the crayon, then wipe off with a paper towel. Test first in an inconspicuous area. If WD-40™ is not available, substitute non-gel toothpaste. Rub over stain, let stand 15 minutes, then wipe off. Repeat as needed.

2. Sponge the stain with dishwashing liquid and hot water.

3. Rinse with water.

113. 📷 **GLUE, MODEL AIRPLANE**

General
Description:

A strong liquid adhesive especially conducive to bonding with plastic pieces. Model-airplane cement is a solvent-type adhesive, which is actually a welding agent. It dissolves the plastics to be bonded, allowing them to join and weld before the solvent evaporates.

Season:

Model-airplane enthusiasts, usually preteenage boys and retired men, are particularly active during periods of free time and they are confined to home. Therefore, stains from this type of glue are most common during cold winter months when recreation is best kept indoors.

Areas of Occurrence:

Those who engage in the precision work of building model airplanes rarely experience gluing accidents. However, there are times when concentration is so intense that glue spills onto a tabletop, carpet, even shirts or pants. In extreme cases, elbows or shirt cuffs end up stuck to a tabletop or other surface.

Time of Occurrence:

Though building model airplanes is an activity probably best left to daylight hours, when you are most likely to be completely alert, those who practice this hobby might find themselves working on a wing or a fuselage well into the wee hours. It is at these times when the potential for stain is greatest.

REMOVAL:

1. **Blot stain with nail polish remover containing acetone, or with straight acetone. Test first for colorfastness. Do not use acetone on acetate materials or silk.**

2. **Rinse well.**

3. Repeat steps 1 and 2 until you have removed as much stain as possible.

 4. Launder according to garment label.

---

114. **GLUE, RUBBER CEMENT**

General Description: *A viscous, flammable liquid consisting of unvulcanized rubber dispersed in benzene, gasoline, or the like, which is used chiefly as an adhesive.* Perhaps most people will remember rubber cement from grade school, where making "boogies" out of the stuff was thought to be a great prank. In fact, rubber cement's consistency is such that its stains are not as irksome as those from regular glue. Rubber cement has a low tension, an advantage when you want to peel something off for repositioning during the adhering process. If the rubber cement is allowed to dry on both surfaces before they are joined, however, the bond is permanent.

Season: Though adults may find uses for rubber cement on occasion, schoolchildren are the primary users of this substance. Stains are thus most likely encountered during the school year.

Areas of Occurrence: The lap area of trousers and jeans as well as the fronts of jumpers, shirts, sweaters, and jackets are candidates for this stain. Luckily, unlike other glues, rubber cement is very thick, cutting down on its ability to run down clothing and spread the stain.

Time of Occurrence:
The hours between 9 A.M. and 3 P.M. are the most likely times for this stain to occur. Occasionally, during the preparation of a project for a science fair or art class, a child may cause a rubber-cement stain after school or in the evening.

REMOVAL:

1. Use a dull knife or spoon to remove as much as possible.

2. Rub petroleum jelly into the stain and roll off as many glue pieces as possible.

3. Rub dishwashing liquid into the stain.

 4. Rinse in warm water.

5. Try to peel or scrape excess glue off.

6. Repeat steps 2 through 5 until no more glue can be removed.

 7. Launder in the hottest water safe for the fabric.

115. **GLUE, WATER-BASED**

General
Description:

A strong liquid adhesive, sometimes made with animal parts. Used for everything from kids' craft projects to postage stamps, this kind of glue can be found in any number of places. Although some glue is made from horses' hooves, in Israel, the glue on postage stamps is certified kosher. Those with dietary concerns of a different nature can be at ease when licking stamps in the United States—there is no more than one tenth of a calorie's worth of glue on every U.S. Postal Service stamp.

Season:

Glue has its purposes year-round—it certainly has a significant presence at any crafts function at camp and school, and even at home when making collages and holiday cards with a personal touch.

Areas of
Occurrence:

Glue stains present themselves in any number of areas—shirts, shorts, pants, and uniforms are all vulnerable at one point or another. The collar and cuff areas of shirts may be at increased risk when worn by a child with an affinity for tasting and perhaps even eating the glue or paste in his elementary school classroom.

Variations of
Significance:

Paste; glue stick

REMOVAL: I. **Use a dull knife or spoon to remove as much as possible.**

2. Rub petroleum jelly into the stain and roll off as many glue pieces as possible.

3. Rub dishwashing liquid into the stain.

4. Rinse in warm water.

5. Try to peel or scrape excess glue off.

6. Repeat steps 2 through 5 until no more glue can be removed.

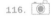

7. Launder in the hottest water safe for the fabric.

---

116. **INK, BALLPOINT**

General Description:

Semisolid substance used for writing or printing, contained in a cartridge inside a pen in which the point is a fine ball bearing that rotates against the ink supply. To most of the world, Biro is still the generic name for the ballpoint pen; it is named after its creator, Hungarian-born journalist Laszlo Josef Biro. Laszlo and his brother George patented the Biro pen in 1938. When ballpoint pens were first sold in 1945, they were priced at a whopping $12 apiece. Nowadays, ballpoint pens are the least expensive, though still the most popular of all writing implements available.

Season:

Most people need to write every day, all year long, thus a stain incurred from the ink in ballpoints may appear at the home or the office—or in the car or outside—any day of they year.

Areas of
Occurrence:

The knees of jeans seem to be popular spots for a line of blue ink; some students might even intentionally put ink on their clothing, especially within the confines of junior high school. Another spot ink stains are generally found is on or around the breast pockets of dress shirts and suit jackets, due to the predilection of ballpoints to leak or break in the pocket. Ink spots may also be found on desks, tables, and walls.

Time of
Occurrence:

There is no time of day or night when a staining of ink in a ballpoint pen will not occur. Homework, letter-writing, and poetry are activities that take place in the afternoon or the middle of the night, or any other time of day when students or authors are so motivated.

REMOVAL: *On fabric:*

1. **Lay the item stain-down on an absorbent material, such as a paper towel. Soak the back of the stain with rubbing alcohol. This will push the stain through the fabric. Blot frequently.**

   2. **Rinse well.**

3. If the stain remains, repeat process with an alcohol-based hairspray (spray the back of the stain), nail polish remover, or turpentine until you find the right method.

4. Rinse well after each treatment.

5. Rub a liquid enzyme detergent into the stain and let stand several minutes.

6. Launder according to garment label.

On a hard surface, such as wood, paneling, or tile:

1. Wipe with damp cloth or sponge.

2. If the stain remains, wipe with rubbing alcohol or nail polish remover.

3. Rinse surface with water.

---

117. **INK, PERMANENT**

General
Description:

A non-removable, non-erasable fluid used for writing or printing. Permanent ink creates stains that are difficult indeed—the substance's very existence depends upon its tenacity. Lab workers can spend years developing formulas that will be absolutely indelible, and marketing copy highlights this feature as the selling-point that will make consumers part with their money.

Season: Permanent ink is a stain without season—it is not bound by weather or month. You may notice an increased risk during the summer months, when you are more likely to label boxes for a move or make signs advertising a yard or garage sale.

Areas of Occurrence: Shirts, especially sleeves and cuffs, as well as pants are prime targets for this difficult stain.

Time of Occurrence: Ink stains are probable at any time indelible ink pens are in use—most likely during daylight hours.

Special Note: This stain needs immediate treatment. Check the ink manufacturer to see if a particular solvent is recommended; use this before employing the stain removal steps that follow.

REMOVAL: *On fabric:*

1. **Place fabric on absorbent cloth and blot the stain with rubbing alcohol. Replace cloth underneath as it becomes saturated with alcohol and ink. Continue until no more ink can be removed.**

2. **Rinse well.**

3. If the stain remains, blot with either acetone (except on acetates) or turpentine. Test first for colorfastness. Replace cloth underneath as it becomes saturated with acetone and ink. Continue until no more ink can be removed.

 4. Rinse well.

 5. Apply a laundry presoak (spot stain remover) and let stand several minutes.

 6. Launder according to garment label.

7. If the stain remains, soak in milk or rub it with white, non-gel toothpaste.

8. Rinse well.

9. Repeat steps 7 and 8 as needed.

 10. Apply a laundry presoak (spot stain remover) and let stand several minutes.

 11. Launder according to garment label.

On a hard surface, such as wood, paneling, or tile:

1. Dampen a cloth with nail polish remover or rubbing alcohol and wipe stain.

2.   Rinse surface with water.

3.   Repeat steps 1 and 2 as needed.

118.   **INK, WATER-BASED**

General
Description:

A fluid used for writing or printing that is made from a base of water with tint added. Water-based ink is the easiest type of ink to remove from clothing and skin, but doesn't have the varied uses that permanent ink does. It is often used in marking pens, and comes in a variety of colors.

Season:

Art projects are assigned year-round, therefore the incidence of these stains will not increase during any particular time of year.

Areas of
Occurrence:

The most common place you see water-based ink stains is on the fingers and hands of someone who has recently completed a drawing or created a home-made birthday card. This substance will easily find its way from the hands onto clothing; the lap areas of jeans and slacks as well as the sleeves and fronts of T-shirts, turtlenecks, and sweaters are the most vulnerable. Other places this stain is likely to appear include tabletops, desks, chairs, walls, and tile flooring.

REMOVAL: *On fabric:*

1. Lay the stain down on an absorbent paper towel. Soak another clean white cloth in rubbing alcohol and dab the other side of the stain. (You can also use water in place of alcohol; use whichever removes the most ink.) Replace the cloth underneath if it becomes soaked. Repeat until you have removed as much ink as possible.

2. Rinse the back of the stain well with water.

3. Rub a liquid laundry detergent into the stain and let stand several minutes.

4. Launder the fabric in the hottest water safe for the fabric.

5. If the stain does not disappear completely, repeat steps 1 through 3, then place item in direct sunlight for several hours to bleach remaining color.

On a hard surface, such as wood, paneling, or tile:

1. Wipe with damp cloth or sponge.

2. If the stain remains, wipe with rubbing alcohol or nail polish remover.

3. **Rinse surface with water.**

119. **PENCIL**

General
Description:

A slender tube of wood, metal, or plastic, containing a core or strip of graphite, a solid coloring material, or the like, used for writing or drawing. Pencils are the implements children use when learning to write letters and numbes; from preschool into adulthood, a pencil is the tool of choice when completing an assignment like a test, a math problem, a drawing, a crossword puzzle, or any other task that may require erasure. In contemporary times, most pencils come equipped with a bit of pink rubber on the top; before this was a common practice, pieces of bread were used to erase lead pencil.

Season:

Pencil stains are without a doubt most common during the months when children are in school. Teachers, students, and even parents may find themselves unwitting victims of this stain. During these months there is a heightened risk at the time of standardized testing, when the use of a number 2 pencil is always required.

Areas of
Occurrence:

Stray pencil markings can stain school uniforms, pockets, or backpacks. Engineers' or editors' shirt pockets are high-risk areas as well. Beware of the pencil sharpener—this nasty devise will spread pencil shavings and, in turn, pencil stains to seemingly unreachable areas, such as socks and pant cuffs.

Time of
Occurrence:
Pencil stains are wily—they belong to the class of stains wherein the victim might not discover his misfortune for hours, or perhaps even days, after the event, especially when the affected area is inside a book bag or purse.

REMOVAL:

1. **Erase gently with a clean eraser.**

2. **If the stain remains, apply a laundry presoak (spot stain remover).**

3. **Launder according to garment label.**

Glossary

Absorbent Cloth:
A material, such as paper towel, sponge, or terry cloth (washcloth), that collects excess stain and liquid. Select a cloth that does not have added perfumes or dyes if possible.

Absorbent Powder:
A powder, such as talcum powder, baking soda, cornstarch, and salt, that absorbs excess liquid from grease and other stains.

Acetone:
A liquid solvent that is helpful in treating nail polish and correction fluid stains. Acetone-based nail polish remover is a readily available form of this solvent. Never use acetone on acetate materials. Test before applying. Caution: Use according to manufacturer's directions. Available: drugstore, hardware store, grocery store

Alcohol, Rubbing (or Isopropyl):
A liquid solvent that is helpful in removing ballpoint ink, chalk, and grass stains. Test before applying. Caution: Use according to manufacturer's directions. Available: drugstore, grocery store

Ammonia:
A colorless gas that is easily absorbed by water; it is sold diluted in water. Helpful in restoring color damaged by bleaches, as well as in treating vinegar stains. Test before applying; generally not safe for silks and wools. Caution: Use according to manufacturer's directions. Available: drugstore, grocery store

Baking Soda (bicarbonate of soda):
An absorbent powder that is nontoxic and nonabrasive. It is often combined with water to form an absorbent paste and is good for treating greasy stains. Available: grocery store

Bar or Natural Soap:	Any white bathroom soap. Select brands without added moisturizers, perfumes, and dyes. Using a bar or natural soap can set certain stains; read all directions thoroughly. Available: drugstore, grocery store
Bleach:	Generally a chemical that removes most color stains. Mild bleaches include white vinegar, lemon juice, hydrogen peroxide, and sunlight. Stronger bleaches, which are readily available and are labeled as "bleach," may contain fabric-weakening chlorine and should be used as a last resort. Chlorine bleach is generally not safe for wool and silk. Test first for colorfastness. Non-chlorine bleaches are also available. Caution: Use according to manufacturer's directions. Available: drugstore, grocery store, natural-food stores
Blot:	To dry or soak up with an absorbent cloth. When blotting a stain with water or other cleaning agent, always blot from the outside edge of the stain and work into the center. This prevents the stain from spreading and forming rings.
Borax:	A water-soluble powdered mineral with antiseptic, antibacterial, and whitening properties. Also called sodium tetraborate or sodium borate. Available: drugstore, hardware store
Carpet Spotter:	A liquid spray or foaming cream often advertised as a quick carpet cleaner. Caution: Use according to manufacturer's directions. Available: drugstore, grocery store
Cheesecloth:	Thin, loosely woven cotton gauze. Available: grocery store

Club Soda:	Carbonated, unflavored water. Cold water can be used in its place. Note: Club soda is *not* the same as tonic water, which contains sugars that will caramelize and form new stains once heat is applied. Available: grocery store
Cold Water:	Water at the temperature of ice water, or the coldest tap water.
Colorfast:	Having colors or dyes that do not run or bleed. Testing for colorfastness is recommended before using any kind of bleach or strong cleaning product. To test, apply the cleaning agent to an inconspicuous area of the garment, such as an inside seam, and dab with an absorbent cloth. If colors run, do not use the cleaning agent on the garment.
Commercial Dye Remover:	Products that are helpful in restoring colors that have run onto other garments. Caution: Use according to manufacturer's directions. Available: drugstore, grocery store
Cornstarch:	A starchy flour made from corn that can be used as an absorbent powder. Available: grocery store
Dishwashing Liquid:	Any basic dishwashing liquid. Select brands that are phosphate-free and do not have added dyes or perfumes. Available: drugstore, grocery store
Dry-cleaning Fluid:	An oil solvent that is helpful in treating oily, greasy stains and is safe for nonwashables. Caution: Use according to manufacturer's directions. Available: drugstore

Enzyme Detergent:	A laundry detergent containing enzymes that "eat" protein stains. Enzyme detergents are also called "digestants." Note: Materials such as wool and silk are proteins, so never use enzyme detergents on these fibers. Available: drugstore, grocery store, natural-food store
Eucalyptus Oil:	Oil derived from the eucalyptus plant. Test before applying. Available: drugstore, natural-food store
Glycerin:	A naturally produced emollient made synthetically or from plant or animal sources, which can be found in liquid or solid form. Available: drugstore, natural-food stores
Hot Water:	Water at a temperature at which you cannot comfortably keep your hand submerged. Never use hot water on protein stains; the heat can set them.
Hydrogen Peroxide (3%):	A mild bleach. Test first for colorfastness. Hydrogen peroxide loses strength over time and when exposed to sunlight, so purchase in small quantities and keep in a cabinet. Available: drugstore, grocery store
Laundry Presoak:	A spot stain remover applied prior to laundering; sold as a liquid, gel, or solid stick. Available: drugstore, grocery store, natural food store
Lemon Juice:	A mild bleach. Test first for colorfastness. Available: grocery store

Laundry Detergent:	Any basic laundry cleanser. Select phosphate-free brands that do not have added dyes and perfumes. Available: drugstore, grocery store, natural-food store
Lukewarm Water:	Water you can comfortably keep your hand in; typically the temperature of bathwater or tepid water.
Meat Tenderizer:	A powder that contains enzymes that help break down proteins. Available: grocery store
Nail Polish Remover:	A mild solvent. Select brands without added dyes or perfumes. Available: drugstore
Non-gel Toothpaste:	A pasty toothpaste that can serve as an absorbent powder when applied to a stain. Available: drugstore, grocery store, natural-food store
Oily Lubricant:	Car-part lubricant that is helpful in "loosening" stains or solids from fabric. Caution: Use according to manufacturer's directions. Available: hardware store
Paint and Varnish Remover:	A solvent used to remove acrylic- and oil-based paint stains. Select an odorless brand. Caution: Use according to manufacturer's directions. Available: hardware store
Rinse:	To flush the back of a stain with water to remove as much of a staining or cleaning agent as possible. If water temperature is not clearly stated in stain removal directions, use lukewarm water. Never rinse with hot water unless stated in directions.

Rust Remover:	A liquid solvent that is helpful in removing rust stains and some dirt or mud stains. Caution: Use according to manufacturer's directions. Available: hardware store
Solution:	A mixture of two or more substances. For example, liquid laundry detergent and water form a *solution*.
Solvent:	A material, like water, that is capable of dissolving another substance.
Sponge:	To moisten with an absorbent cloth.
Talcum Powder:	An absorbent powder that is helpful in treating ointment, salad dressing, and other greasy stains. Available: drugstore, grocery store
Tile Cleaner:	Liquid or foaming product for use in the bathroom. Caution: Use according to manufacturer's directions. Available: drugstore, grocery store, natural-food store
Turpentine:	A solvent derived from pine oil that is used as a thinner for tough grease stains such as tar and asphalt, as well as for oil-based paints. Caution: Use according to manufacturer's directions. Available: hardware store
Vinegar, White:	A solution of 5 percent acetic acid that can be used as a mild bleach. Test first for colorfastness. Available: grocery store

Index

Numbers in **bold** (for example, **108**) are stain numbers, and can be used to locate stains in the photograph section. All other numbers are page numbers.